101 Best Ways
To Get Ahead

101 Best Ways To Get Ahead

Solid Gold Advice from 101 of the World's Most Successful People

Written by Michael Angier
with Sarah Pond

Cover design by Michael Angier

Published by
Success Networks International, Inc.
Win-Win Way, PO Box 2048
South Burlington, Vermont 05407-2048
www.SuccessNet.org

Table of Contents

Acclaim

"This is a great book, full of powerful, practical ideas you can apply immediately to improve your life."

—Brian Tracy
author of *Getting Rich Your Own Way*
www.BrianTracy.com

". . . . one of the most important books you will ever read . . . a collection of 101 of the most powerful ideas in the history of civilization!*"*

—Dr. Phil Humbert
author of *Alive, Awake & Aware!*
www.PhilipHumbert.com

"Michael Angier's 101 Best Ways to Get Ahead *is an absolute dynamite display of powerful success principles all wrapped up in one book. Tap into the immense knowledge in this ebook and put it into action! You'll be incredibly glad you did."*

Mike Litman
co-author of *Conversations with Millionaires*
www.MikeLitman.com

"This book is a treasure trove of wisdom, filled with great advice and inspiring stories of smart, savvy, successful people from all walks of life. Don't just read this book; devour it. Return to it over and over for motivation, inspiration and activation. This is not just another self-help book. It's an action plan for life. Thank you, Michael, for gifting us these pearls of wisdom."

—Mitch Axelrod
author of *The NEW Game of Business*
www.TheNewGame.com

"Michael Angier has created the definitive how-to book for the successful dreamer. With this book and a few ounces of ambition, there isn't a creative goal out there that couldn't be mastered happily and efficiently."

—Suzanne Falter-Barns
best-selling author
www.HowMuchJoy.com

"Wow! The wisdom of the true masters of success all wrapped up in a read that has you reeling with the feeling of total empowerment and for less than dinner for two. Great job, guys!"

—Rick Beneteau
award-winning author and creator of the blockbuster eBook
Success: A Spiritual Matter
www.OnlyGoodBusiness.com

"What a priceless collection! I quickly skimmed it and kept stopping at true words of wisdom. There is something here for everyone, no matter your mood or your profession. I love it!"

—Joe Vitale
author of too many books to list here,
including the forthcoming "The Attractor Factor"
www.MrFire.com

"If you only read one book this year, this should be it! You won't find a more powerful, concise, and useful collection of real-world success advice anywhere. It gets right to the point and delivers only the best of the best. The bar has just been raised on self-development literature worldwide. No success library is complete without this book. Should be required reading for everyone on the planet!"

—Sterling Valentine
Fortune 500 Marketing Coach and author of
Mastering Your Marketing: How to Effortlessly Attract All the Clients You Deserve
www.SterlingValentine.com

"101 Best Ways to Get Ahead is a jewel! Each one of the 'Ways' is short, concise, crisp and clear! Each has an Action Point so you can turn wisdom into reality fast! And wisdom isn't all you get—the second half of the book profiles the 101 people who contributed to it, and is connected to web sites, articles and additional relevant material about that luminary. Looking for a mentor, a model, a teacher? Follow the links through and find out even more about what successful people think about, do and believe. A hearty Thank You to Michael Angier and Sarah Pond for distilling the wisdom of so many of our contemporary heroes and 'she-roes' and making it so easy to access. A job well done!"

—JoAnna Brandi
The Customer Care Coach®,
author of *Winning at Customer Retention, Building Customer Loyalty* and several others
www.CustomerCareCoach.com

"I've heard it said, 'Beware the man who offers you new fundamentals. There are none. Fundamentals take time to get that way.' Well, success guru Michael Angier has taken that advice to heart and compiled a list of 101 Success Fundamentals that are sure-fire, time-tested ways to get ahead. Michael and his team have combed the public record for simple, powerful and far-reaching wisdom anyone can use to improve their lot. My advice? Pick one idea each day and find some way to apply it—in three months you'll be so much farther ahead, you won't believe it."

—Paul Lemberg
president, Quantum Growth Coaching Franchise
www.QuantumGrowthCoachingFranchise.com
www.PaulLemberg.com

"Michael and Sarah have compiled a rich resource of both inspiration and practical advice, all easily accessible in 101 Best Ways to Get Ahead. *It is unique in that it offers pithy advice delivered straight up, followed by inspiring mini biographies of some of the most fascinating and successful people alive today. This book is user friendly because of the way it is organized to value the reader's time, i.e., you can go directly to the subject of your interest and find timeless wisdom to guide you on your way to getting ahead."*

—Paul Cutright
best-selling co-author of *You're Never Upset for the Reason You Think*
www.YoureNeverUpset.com

"Warning! This eBook will change your life! The sage advice of 101 of the most note-worthy individuals living in the world today and picked by those of us who aspire to leave legacies ourselves! Wow! As a former educator, one of the items that I really like about this eBook is that it is not just another eBook filled with information to clutter our minds. No way! This eBook is written with the student in mind. It delivers information screened by personal experiences. It delivers knowledge, skills and attitudes! It is truly a masterpiece for those who are students of personal and professional success. For me, the bottom-line criteria for a successful eBook is that it compels the reader into action. This eBook does that! And it does so in a way for the reader to meaningfully and personally reflect.

Read it, and more importantly, take action on its advice. What you will find yourself doing is using it to launch you into focused, outcome-driven action. And, of course, action is the ultimate answer to moving your life forward—both personally and professionally! I whole-heartedly recommend this eBook. You won't be disappointed!"

—Glenn Dietzel
*author of an eBook in Record Time and Build Multiple
Streams of Income With a Proven, Breakthrough System*
www.AwakenTheAuthorWithin.com

"This extraordinary book is going to be around for a long, long time. Actually, it has the feel of a true success-inspiring classic. This is real advice by many of the most awesome leaders in today's world. Copies of 101 Best Ways to Get Ahead *will continue to live on the 'inspiration' corner of my desk, by my bedside, and on my family and special friends gift-list."*

—Dr. Jill Ammon-Wexler
author of Take Charge: 14 Steps to Smash Your Limits
www.Quantum-self.com

"The best way I've found to read this book is to clear my mind, focus on my goal, then open the book to where I'm guided; and live my day following the action step that Michael has so succinctly summarized. Michael's drive and passion for understanding and living what consti-tutes the successful life shines brightly through all these pages.
Thanks, Michael, for gathering this essential knowledge all in one place."

—Gurusahay Khalsa, D.C, Dipl.Ac.
author and lecturer on health and healing
www.GrdHealth.com

"WOW! A Lifetime of Timeless Wisdom in One Powerful Little Book! I was really excited when I heard about this book. With all the so-called guru's out there it's hard to know who to trust. What's cool about 101 Best Ways to Get Ahead *is that you get to see inside the heads of the world's most influential people—people who have changed the face of history. And to learn firsthand the powerful lessons that shaped these people was exhilarating. I mean, I couldn't put it down. Read it and you'll see. People will be talking about this book for years to come. I know I will!"*

—Kristie T
author, speaker, consultant
www.KristieT.com

About the Authors

Michael Angier is the founder and CIO (Chief Inspiration Officer) of SuccessNet, the popular web-based community dedicated to helping people operate at their personal and professional best.

Michael is a father, husband, mentor, author, speaker, entrepreneur, coach and student. He's also the creator of The World Class Business™ Conference and has taught seminars and conducted workshops on goal setting, motivation and personal development in four countries.

Michael's passion is human potential. Helping people discover, develop and fulfill their dreams is his purpose, which is clearly reflected in SuccessNet. Michael is one of those individuals who has found his purpose in life and aligns all his endeavors with it.

Intrigued by the science of individual achievement early in his life, Michael has devoted himself to advancing his experience and expertise in personal and professional development for more than 30 years.

In his youth, already an ardent student of the principles of success, Michael began reading biographies of successful individuals and was fascinated by their lives and the contributions they made to the world. Likely, that interest was the seed for the project that resulted in the book you're reading right now.

Michael is married to Dawn Angier—his partner, best friend, mentor, teacher, student and confidante. They live in South Burlington, Vermont and have six children ranging in age from 13 to 33. Michael enjoys sailing, tennis, traveling, reading and helping people realize their dreams.

Sarah Pond works closely with Michael as SuccessNet's director of membership services and is the in-house creative maximizer. Trained as a life coach and experienced as a speaker and workshop facilitator, Sarah also produces self-development products and resources.

Sarah has combined her passion for self-evolution helping others with her aptitude for the written word. The result is a home-based business that dovetails perfectly with her lifestyle.

Sarah is married to the man of her dreams, Steve, an elementary school teacher. She loves her down-shifted life in seaside Halfmoon Bay, British Columbia. She relaxes while reading, writing, gardening and renovating.

Acknowledgements

The "101 Most Successful People" were generous with their time and their advice. We're thankful for their contribution and their cooperation.

The subscribers and members of SuccessNet provided the fertile ground for this book to grow. Without their participation in the original survey, and without the vast global network that we've created over the last nine years, we would not have had the time, the money or the belief to make it happen.

We're grateful to Dawn Angier for her support, her encouragement, her ideas and her excellent copy editing and proofing. We couldn't have done it without her.

Our Master Mind partners believed in the project from the beginning. At every meeting, they asked how it was going and offered ideas, direction and encouragement. Thank you.

We sincerely appreciate the people to whom we sent review copies and who then gave us their feedback, testimonials and endorsements. Their assistance not only provided us with a different perspective, but also validation, encouragement and valuable tools for marketing this work.

This was the largest project Sarah and I have worked on. And it won't be the last. It was an absolute pleasure to work with her. Her talent and professionalism made the job easy. We make a great team.

We're grateful to people everywhere working to achieve their full and unique potential. And to those who contribute something to the betterment of the world—with their time, their love, their care and their talents.

Tribute to President Ronald Reagan

Ronald Reagan ended up near the top of the list of the original "101 Most Successful People Living Today." As we began writing this book, Ronald Reagan passed away after battling Alzheimer's for ten years.

It seemed fitting to dedicate *101 Best Ways to Get Ahead* to this great man because he believed in and embodied much of the practical wisdom this book contains.

During the state and private funeral services this past summer, we honored one of the most respected presidents the United States has had. I was happily surprised at just how *much* respect and honor was paid to our 40th president.

And it wasn't only to his accomplishments—of which there were many—it was to the man himself. Among other things, he was kind, he was jovial, he was dignified, he was fair. Regardless whether you agreed with his politics, you couldn't help but admire his goodness and his success.

To have it said that the world was a far better place because you have lived is the highest compliment one can earn. We can certainly say this was true of Ronald Wilson Reagan.

Our flags flew at half-staff for a month, and our hearts were full of pride, of sadness and respect. Thank you, President Reagan. Thank you for your service. Thank you for your leadership. Thank you for your optimism. Thank you for your values. Thank you for your

> "No arsenal or no weapon in the arsenals of the world is so formidable as the will and moral courage of free men and women."
> —Ronald Reagan

principles. Thank you for your vision. And thank you for being a shining example of so much of what's good in the world.

We are proud to dedicate *101 Best Ways to Get Ahead* to the life and the memory of President Ronald Reagan.

—Michael Angier

Foreword by Dr. Phil Humbert

Congratulations on purchasing one of the most important books you will ever read!

I know that may seem like a grandiose claim, but as they say, "It ain't braggin' if you can do it," and the book you hold in your hands can, and will, more than fulfill its promise. How do I know? Because I've seen these ideas work. I've seen them transform lives. I've seen the power they hold—and that you now hold in your hands—to make a difference!

Here are three key ideas that are the foundation for this book. Together they form the foundation for all success in life:

1. Success begins and is created with ideas. Wilbur and Orville Wright *imagined* the airplane before they built it. Werner Von Braun imagined going to the moon fifty years before Neil Armstrong radioed back, "That's one small step for man, one giant leap for mankind."

    Albert Einstein said that "imagination rules the world" because ideas come first. You hold in your hand a book of the most important ideas and solutions ever collected in one place. No wonder I began by saying, "Congratulations!"

2. Success is based on a set of skills and behaviors. Success, whether in the world of business or parenting or spiritual peace, is not based on luck or chance or coincidence. No. We live in a world of cause-and-effect. Success is built on skills and actions, and that is a *glorious* truth!

3. Skills, ideas, behaviors and attitudes can be learned. There was a time you could not walk; now you can. There was a time you could not read; now you can. There was a time when learning the skills and behaviors of the world's most successful people was difficult or impossible; now you hold in your hands a collection of 101 of the *most powerful ideas in the history of civilization!*

From the beginning of time, successful people have learned from the success of others. Napoleon Hill, Earl Nightingale, James Brown, Marianne Williamson, Oprah Winfrey and thousands of others have recommended that we "learn from the masters."

Now, you can. Read this book. Take notes in the margins, copy the important ideas and carry them in your pocket or paste them on your computer. Ponder them. Try the ideas, practice the skills, and where necessary, modify them for your particular circumstance. But here is the key: I absolutely promise that if you "do the things successful people do, you will get the results that successful people get."

While I didn't write this book, I wish I had. Since I didn't write it, it may seem presumptuous for me to thank you for buying it, but I believe in the potential of every human being, and I'm excited to see the impact this book will have. As a coach, I love seeing people achieve their dreams and fulfill their destiny. So I thank you for buying this book, and I urge you to use it to create the life you truly want.

Best wishes, and I'll see you at the top!

Philip E. Humbert, PhD
www.PhilipHumbert.com

Introduction

How and Why this Book Came into Being

In the spring of 2004, we had an idea. It started as a spark, a lingering question: What advice would the most successful people in the world have for us? And just who *are* the most successful people living today?

That spark became a flame as we pursued the idea. We got excited about obtaining such wise advice and sharing it with others. We envisioned the impact of that wisdom on the lives of those who acted upon it. Soon the flame burned brighter as the vision grew stronger.

We imagined a whole group of successful men and women sharing their best advice on how to get ahead in the world. We saw how thousands of lives could be transformed by it.

The project was launched, and the book began to take form.

The "101 Most Successful" were determined by a survey of our readers—over 80,000. We received 1,794 responses. The "101 Most Successful" may not all be names you or I might select. It's likely that some of the people who were voted as most successful were more *famous* than successful.

If you're looking for negatives about these people, you won't find it here. It was our intention to talk about what they're known for and why what they have to say should be considered.

Regardless of whether each one of these 101 would be *your* pick, there's solid, helpful and profound advice you can use to help you get ahead in the world.

Here's the question we asked of our "101 Most Successful People":

> *"What advice would you give a son, daughter or grandchild? Based upon your knowledge and experience, what would you share with them that would be most helpful to them getting along and getting ahead in the world?"*

And they told us.

This book is about these distinguished people, but it's also about *you*. You can learn something about these people, but you can learn a lot more about how to live more effectively—how to be more successful—how to be your best, both personally and professionally.

And now—with this book—you have access to the best advice from some of the best minds.

Not all of the "101 Most Successful" were able or willing to participate. Some were restricted by current publishing contracts. In a few cases, we were unable to contact them. With them, we read their books, we reviewed their speeches, and we researched their values and their beliefs to extract their wisdom.

As you can imagine, much advice from our "101 Most Successful" was similar. Rather than attempt to attribute each piece of advice to the specific person or persons who gave it, we elected to summarize each piece of advice without always assigning it to a particular person.

"The 101 Most Successful" often used quotes from others to make their point, and we've included many of those quotes here. Even in instances where we quoted from one of The 101, there may have been others who offered the same or similar guidance. The intention was to provide the best recommendations in as concise and as digestible a format as we could.

The Process
We had a lot of fun doing this project. It was cool to watch the expression of the postal worker when we handed her the packages being sent to The Queen of England, President Bush, Tony Blair, The Pope and others. It was also fun to receive responses from The 101.

What You Do with It
The rest is up to you. How will you apply this sage advice? If you follow much of this counsel on a consistent basis, you may very well one day find yourself on a list of "101 Most Successful People."

And even if you don't become as well known or as successful as the people on our 101 list, you'll have achieved far more, become much more and served many more than you would have otherwise.

—Michael Angier

How to Use This Book

101 Best Ways to Get Ahead is not a book to be read in one sitting. To do so would be like trying to take a sip of water from a fire hose.

Instead, the wisdom it contains should be savored and enjoyed. It's meant to be read for brief periods in order that you might reflect upon what you've read and begin to apply it in your life. Pick out a few advice nuggets and focus on them for a week at a time.

Another idea is to rate yourself on each of the recommendations. On a scale of 1 to 10, how do you see yourself in exemplifying each of these chunks of wisdom?

You may be tempted to discount some of the advice because it seems trite or simplistic. Indeed, some of the advice may sound a bit like a cliché. But is it a cliché because it's common or is it a cliché because it's true? We didn't include anything because it was common; we included it because it works.

Keep *101 Ways to Get Ahead* handy. Keep it by your nightstand or your favorite chair where you can pick it up and read for a few moments at a time.

We encourage you to buy a copy of this book for those people you care about. Think of the contribution you could make to a young person's life by giving them the pearls of wisdom this book contains.

Talk about these ideas with others. Use the advice to prompt a discussion with friends, family or coworkers. In doing so, you'll gain the full value of your investment and be well on *your* way to being one of the world's most successful people.

Here are some questions to consider when reading or discussing these golden nuggets of advice:

- ☑ How does this fit for me?
- ☑ How closely do I follow this advice?
- ☑ Who do I know that best emulates this strategy or concept?
- ☑ What can I do today to begin making this work for me?
- ☑ Where can I get the skills, experience or knowledge to make this true in my life?

Icons in This Book

As you read this book, you'll notice special graphics. These are icons to help emphasize action points and resources.

Action Points

With each item, we've suggested steps you can take to help you begin to incorporate these important concepts into your life. They're simply meant to get you thinking about what to do next—to move you toward your highest and best.

Resources

Throughout this book, we've also included links to other resources that will be helpful in gaining additional tools, information, ideas and support related to the subject.

The 101 Most Successful
and Respected People Living Today

Listed in order of popularity. *(A few of our "101 Most Successful" received tied rankings. We chose to randomly list them within their ranking.)*

1. Bill Gates - Microsoft founder, philanthropist
2. Oprah Winfrey - The Oprah Winfrey Show
3. Dr. Nelson Mandela - South Africa president
4. George W. Bush - U.S. president
5. Jimmy Carter - former U.S. president
6. Warren Buffet - investor, author, philanthropist
7. Donald Trump - real estate mogul
8. Anthony Robbins - speaker, author
9. Stephen Covey - author, consultant
10. Pope John Paul II - Catholic pope
11. Bill Clinton - former U.S. president
12. Hillary Clinton - U.S. senator
13. Dr. Wayne Dyer - author, speaker
14. The Dalai Lama - spiritual leader
15. Jim Rohn - speaker, author
16. Dr. Billy Graham - Christian evangelist
17. Dr. Deepak Chopra - speaker, author
18. Zig Ziglar - speaker, author
19. Richard Branson - entrepreneur, adventurer
20. Colin Powell - U.S. secretary of state
21. Maya Angelou - author, poet
22. Margaret Thatcher - former U.K. prime minister
23. Jack Welch - former General Electric president
24. Kofi Annan - UN secretary-general
25. Dr. Phil McGraw - author, speaker, The Dr. Phil Show
26. Steven Spielberg - movie director
27. Tiger Woods - golf champion
28. Dr. John C. Maxwell – speaker, author
29. Mark Victor Hansen - speaker, author
30. Rudy Giuliani - former mayor, consultant
31. Arnold Schwarzenegger - California governor, actor

32. Dr. Condoleeza Rice - U.S. national security advisor
33. Michael Jordan - basketball champion
34. Robert Kiyosaki - author
35. Mel Gibson - actor, director, producer
36. Steve Jobs - Apple Computers founder
37. Muhammad Ali - world champion boxer
38. Queen Elizabeth II - Queen of England
39. Bono - entertainer, activist
40. Brian Tracy - speaker, author
41. Christopher Reeve - actor, activist *(died October 10, 2004)*
42. Lance Armstrong - bicycle racing champion
43. Madonna – entertainer, author
44. Paul McCartney - singer, songwriter
45. Paul Newman - actor, philanthropist
46. Robert Allen - author
47. Tony Blair – United Kingdom prime minister
48. Barbara Walters - journalist
49. Marianne Williamson - author
50. Michael Dell - Dell Computers founder
51. Dr. Robert Schuller - Christian pastor, author
52. Stephen King - author
53. John McCain - U.S. senator
54. Tom Peters - author, speaker
55. Bill Cosby - comedian, actor
56. JK Rowling - author
57. Anita Roddick - The Body Shop founder
58. Barbra Streisand - actor, singer
59. Bob Proctor - author, speaker
60. Edward de Bono - author, teacher, lecturer
61. Jay Leno - comedian, late-night talk show host
62. Julia Cameron - artist
63. Katie Couric - journalist
64. Laura Bush - U.S. first lady
65. Madeline Albright - former secretary of state
66. Pelé - soccer champion
67. Dr. Steven Hawking – physicist, author
68. Wayne Gretzky - hockey champion

69. Cheryl Richardson - coach, author, speaker
70. Desmond Tutu - archbishop
71. Dr. Jane Goodall - primatologist
72. Jay Abraham - marketing expert
73. John Grisham - author
74. Mikhail Gorbachev - former Soviet Union president
75. Peter Jackson - movie director
76. Robin Williams - comedian, actor
77. Sean Connery - actor
78. Susan Sarandon - actor, activist
79. Suze Orman - author, finance expert
80. Ted Turner - media mogul
81. Tom Brokaw - TV anchorman
82. Tom Cruise – actor, producer
83. Walter Cronkite - TV anchorman
84. Andre Agassi - tennis champion
85. Barbara Bush - former U.S. first lady
86. Celine Dion - singer
87. David Letterman - comedian, late-night talk show host
88. Gloria Steinem - publisher, activist
89. John Travolta – actor, producer
90. Julia Roberts – actor, producer
91. Lee Iacocca - former Chrysler president
92. Maria Shriver - journalist, author
93. Michael Chrichton - author, screenwriter
94. Dr. Sally Ride - astronaut
95. Elizabeth Dole - U.S. senator
96. Norman Schwarzkopf - U.S. Army general
97. Bob Dole - former U.S. senator
98. Bill O'Reilly - talk show host
99. Meg Whitman - eBay CEO
100. Rupert Murdoch - media mogul
101. Tom Hanks - actor, director

How to Use the Categories

We organized the sage suggestions from our "101 Most Successful" into 12 categories. It will be easier for you to locate advice and dig deeper into the various subjects.

Business & Career

If you ask most people what they think is meant by getting ahead, they will usually think of doing so in their job or business. Our working life seems to take up the largest chunk of our daily lives.

Relationships

Getting ahead in the world requires getting along with others. Our "101 Most Successful" believe that not only are good relationships important in becoming successful, they feel good relationships are part of the wealth of success.

Motivation

All success requires a desire to achieve. Getting motivated, staying motivated and motivating others is an important part of getting ahead in the world.

Money/Finance

Interestingly enough, not a lot of advice was offered from our "101 Most Successful" about money or finance. Do they think so little of money because most of them have so much of it? Or do they have so much of it because they think so little about it?

Creativity

Creativity plays a large role in moving us forward, navigating change and accomplishing our goals. Successful people know this and tap into their creativity to achieve their objectives.

Mission/Vision

Muhammad Ali may have said it best: "Champions aren't made in gyms. Champions are made from something they have deep inside them: A desire, a dream, a vision. They have to have last-minute stamina, they have to be a little faster, they have to have the skill and the will. But the will must be stronger than the skill."

Health
Good health is the first wealth. Without it, all our other success has little value. Becoming and/or remaining healthy should be a critical objective and worthy of our best efforts.

Values
Stephen Covey: "There is no shortcut. But there is a path. The path is based on principles revered throughout history. If there is one message to glean from this wisdom, it is that a meaningful life is not a matter of speed or efficiency. It's much more a matter of what you do and why you do it than how fast you get it done."

Industry/Productivity
By its very definition, all success requires action. Getting things done effectively, efficiently and consistently plays a critical role in how we get along in the world.

Stewardship
Now more than ever, we are called upon to be good stewards. The world has become smaller and is more easily impacted by what we do and what we don't do. Many of our "101 Most Successful" are active in environmental preservation and are concerned about *all* of our resources.

Spirituality
The Dalai Lama: "When we meet real tragedy in life, we can react in two ways—either by losing hope and falling into self-destructive habits or by using the challenge to find our inner strength."

General
Advice in this area either didn't fit into the above categories or was broad enough to be included in most of them. They are still worthy of our study and our attention.

101 Best Ways To Get Ahead

Solid Gold Advice
from 101 of the
World's Most
Successful People

Written by Michael Angier
with Sarah Pond

BUSINESS AND CAREER

If you ask most people what they think is meant by getting ahead, they'll usually think of doing so in their job or business. Our working life takes up that largest chunk of our daily lives. What follows is sound, sage advice on how to advance your career.

1. Invest in Yourself

Jim Rohn says, "Work harder on yourself than you do in your job." He also says, "Formal education will make you a living; self-education will make you a fortune."

> "Success is not to be pursued; it is to be attracted by the person we become."
>
> —Jim Rohn

By dedicating yourself to lifelong learning, there's no limit to how much better you can make yourself. In doing so, you increase the value you bring to the marketplace. As Buckminster Fuller said, "You can't learn less."

Tony Robbins: "If we habitually focus on how to improve things that are already great, can you see how this spirit can transform ourselves, our organizations, families and communities?"

Jack Welch: "The best things workers can bring to their jobs is a lifelong thirst for learning."

Stephen King: "If you don't have the time to read, you don't have the time or the tools to write."

Queen Elizabeth II: "It's all to do with the training; you can do a lot if you're properly trained."

Kofi Annan: "Knowledge is power. Information is liberating. Education is the premise of progress, in every society, in every family."

Improve your mind. Enhance your skills. Increase your knowledge. Read at least an hour a day from books that will help you get better at what you do. Listen to educational audio programs in your car. Attend courses and seminars that give you ideas and insights to help you advance your career.

2. Tell People About Your Success

Donald Trump advises us to be sure to tell others about our successes. He says you can't expect people to find out about your triumphs on their own. You have to make sure they know what you've done.

Many of us allow our humility to get in the way. When this virtue is carried to extremes, it limits our success.

We all know people we find boring, because they're constantly boasting and telling us how great they are. In our attempt to not be like them, we sometimes become overly cautious and "hide our light under a bushel."

This doesn't serve us, and it doesn't serve others. People want to be around people who are doing things and accomplishing things. Shakespeare said it well when he wrote, "a rising tide floats all ships."

The key is to tell about our successes, but do it in a way where we're not just crowing about how great we are. Sharing achievements provides an opportunity to acknowledge those involved in the process. It's news. And people are inspired by great accomplishments. By *not* telling about it, we deprive others of that inspiration.

Everyone would agree that Trump has followed his own advice. Some might even fault him for going a bit too far. But not going far enough may be costing us and our organizations more than we know.

Oprah Winfrey: "Be more splendid, more extraordinary. Use every moment to fill yourself up."

Arnold Schwarzenegger: "I knew I was a winner back in the late sixties. I knew I was destined for great things. People will say that kind of thinking is totally immodest. I agree. Modesty is not a word that applies to me in any way—I hope it never will."

 Document your recent accomplishments and send out a press release. Tell your clients. Tell your staff. Make sure people know the good things you've done.

3. Consistency: The Major Key to Your Success

We live in an age where the desire for instant gratification is common. People expect quick results.

> "If you develop the habits of success, you'll make success a habit."
>
> —Michael Angier

And in some cases, we *do* get results quickly.

However, real, lasting and meaningful success requires sustained and consistent effort. Anyone can diet for a day. Anyone can work hard for brief periods of time. We can take a class to increase our knowledge or generate and act upon a good idea.

But to really produce what we want, we must consistently think and act in productive ways. Sometimes the results come rapidly, but most of the time they come from hanging in there and constantly and religiously practicing the things we need to do.

The same is true for *negative* results. We don't become obese with a one-time, high-fat indulgence. One cigarette probably won't kill us— although it might—and one lapse in judgment will rarely ruin our future.

But sustained and prolonged, unhealthy or counterproductive activities will almost certainly produce catastrophic outcomes.

Consistency is an admired trait in our political leaders—when we can find it. We value consistency in our health care. We require consistency in accounting principles. We appreciate consistency in government. So why should we be any different?

The flash in the pan may be dramatic, but it can't stand up to the constant heat and the resulting success that comes from consistent, steady and reliable efforts.

Colin Powell: "If you are going to achieve excellence in big things, you develop the habit in little matters. Excellence is not an exception, it is a prevailing attitude."

Margaret Thatcher: "You may have to fight a battle more than once to win it."

Brian Tracy: "You have to put in many, many, many tiny efforts that nobody sees or appreciates before you achieve anything worthwhile."

Katie Couric: "It's hard to get up every morning for 10 years, but if you love your work, once you wipe the sleep from your eyes and get in the shower, it just becomes another day."

 What are the things you know you need to do on a consistent basis to accomplish your goals and live an abundant life? Determine the things you're not regularly doing, and decide which ones you're willing to commit to doing every day. Then, stick to it. Your consistency will pay off.

4. Develop a Thick Skin, Soft Heart

And never mix them up. It's good to be kind-hearted. But many kind-hearted people are also tender-hearted. In other words, they're easily hurt by insults, jabs and even teasing remarks.

> "Honest criticism is hard to take, particularly from a relative, a friend, an acquaintance or a stranger."
>
> —Franklin P. Jones

The ability to be unaffected by inconsiderate or misdirected people requires self confidence and a thick skin.

Bill O'Reilly, host of Fox News' *The O'Reilly Factor,* reads a few emails he's received at the end of each show. He shares some of the laudatory ones, but he also shares some of the bitter and mean-spirited ones. The way he handles the latter is a great example of being able to laugh off what Shakespeare called "the slings and arrows of outrageous fortune."

There's an old adage: to avoid criticism, say nothing, do nothing, be nothing. If you want to get ahead in the world, you'll have to do all three. So expect to be criticized.

The trick is to discern what is helpful criticism and what you need to shrug off. If you're never being criticized, judged or disparaged in any way, you're probably not doing all that much, and you need to move up a few notches on the "Go-for-it-Scale."

Margaret Thatcher: "To wear your heart on your sleeve isn't a very good plan; you should wear it inside, where it functions best."

Bill Cosby: "I don't know the key to success, but the key to failure is trying to please everybody."

 Don't let the turkeys get you down. Don't take it personally. Recognize that everyone has their opinion, and you don't always have to defend yours.

If you trust the source—or you're getting the same criticism from several people—consider the validity of their views, and take corrective action when it's warranted. If it's not, thank the person for sharing and forget it. "Let the dogs bark, the caravan moves on."

5. Do What You Love and Love What You Do

If you really want to be successful, feel fulfilled and live a healthy life, it's paramount you truly enjoy the work you do. In order to deliver your greatest value to the world, you must be employed in work that interests you and inspires you.

> "I'd rather be a failure at something I love than a success at something I hate."
>
> —George Burns

Doing work you despise places you out of integrity, and true success will likely forever remain elusive.

Richard Branson: "A business has to be involving, it has to be fun and it has to exercise your creative instincts."

This advice was given to us by more of the "101 Most Successful" than any other. Life is too short to spend it doing something we experience as tedious, uninteresting or lacking in meaning. You'll never fulfill your destiny doing work you despise.

Anita Roddick: "I tried to redefine work as a spiritual endeavor, not just a job, not just a Monday to Friday sort of death."

Warren Buffet: "I love what I do. I'm involved in a kind of intellectually interesting game that isn't too tough to win, and Berkshire Hathaway is my canvas."

Wayne Dyer: "Doing what you love is the cornerstone of having abundance in your life."

 Invest whatever you need in finding your passion. As a popular book title recommended, *Do What You Love, the Money Will Follow.*

6. Live Your Life Like it's an Open Book

In this day and age, your life really *is* an open book. Anything you've done in your lifetime can be investigated. And if you run for public office or seek any leadership position, you can expect that it *will* be.

> "Honesty and transparency make you vulnerable. Be honest and transparent anyway."
>
> —Mother Teresa

Besides, isn't it better to live your life like everything you do will be public? It means less guilt and no fear of being found out. You can never be blackmailed or coerced into doing something you don't want to do.

Billy Graham: "A real Christian is a person who can give his pet parrot to the town gossip."

Tom Hanks: "The only way you can truly control how you're seen is by being honest all the time."

 In everything you do, ask yourself: Would I want others to know what I have done? Would I be proud to have people know about this decision, action or inaction? If you have to answer no, or probably not, you should likely make a new decision.

 Business is All About Relationships
www.SuccessNet.org/members/articles/angier-relationship.htm

7. Know When to Quit

Persistence is a valuable attribute and much success has been attributed to hanging in there when most would have quit.

> "Champions keep playing until they get it right."
> —Billie Jean King

But sometimes, you have to cut your losses. There comes a time when your resources could be better utilized elsewhere. We're not saying this point of departure is an easy one to assess. But when diminishing returns pile up, there are times when throwing in the towel is the best course of action.

Wayne Dyer: "You are doomed to make choices. This is life's greatest paradox."

Maya Angelou: "The need for change bulldozed a road down the center of my mind."

 What are you doing that's no longer worth doing?

8. Cash is King

You can be profitable and still go out of business. And many companies do just that. Booked sales may increase your bottom line, but until funds are collected, you can't pay your expenses.

Cash flow—more specifically a *positive* cash flow—is paramount. Managing cash is critical to your success.

Anita Roddick: "Business is not financial science; it's about trading—buying and selling. It's about creating a product or service so good that people will pay for it."

Steven Spielberg: "Why pay a dollar for a bookmark? Why not use the dollar for a bookmark?"

 Don't get surprised by a shortage of funds. Be sure to have a cash flow projection as well as a Performa P&L. Know when, why and how money will come in as well as when it goes out.

9. Don't Be a Complainer

If you become labeled as a whiner, your career is in trouble. The reason is, no one wants to work with people who complain.

> "Realize that if you have time to whine and complain about something then you have the time to do something about it."
> —Anthony J. D'Angelo

There's a vast difference between someone who calls attention to important problems and someone who complains about the same things and never offers a solution.

Mary Angelou: "If you don't like something, change it. If you can't change it, change your attitude. Don't complain."

Rudy Giuliani: "When you confront a problem, you begin to solve it."

 Resolve to never become a whiner. Work on your attitude. Don't complain about something unless you're prepared to offer a solution.

RELATIONSHIPS

Getting ahead in the world requires getting along with others. Our "101 Most Successful" believe that not only are good relationships important in becoming successful, they feel good relationships are part of the wealth of success.

10. Don't Burn Your Bridges

No one wants enemies. But over a lifetime, most people create some. What we need instead are more allies. And it's up to us whether we create friends or opponents.

> "Friends come and go, but enemies accumulate."
>
> —unknown

> "If you're going to burn your bridges, you'd better become an excellent swimmer."
>
> —Harvey McKay

It's an increasingly smaller world. In days of old, you could move to a new location, change industries, change social contacts and rarely run into an old enemy. Now more than ever, it's important not to create adversaries.

It's unnecessary to create enemies. Not everyone is going to see things your way. But you can disagree with people without being disagreeable. It doesn't cost much to be diplomatic, and it pays very well.

You can expect to be treated unfairly by a number of people in the course of your lifetime. But it's not worth burning your bridges. Sometimes things just don't work out, and it's only human to want to blame someone or something for it. Resist this temptation.

You may even be tempted to prove yourself "right" or to get even. There is rarely a payoff for such tactics—if any at all. We're judged—fairly or unfairly—by how we react and how we treat others in difficult times.

This doesn't mean you have to be a doormat. We certainly don't advocate being a pushover. But you can confront without being combative.

It's a big life. What we're upset about now will rarely have much of an impact on our life—even though it might seem like it now.

Barbara Bush: "Never lose sight of the fact that the most important yardstick of your success will be how you treat other people—your family, friends and coworkers, even strangers you meet along the way."

Billy Graham: "Hot heads and cold hearts never solved anything."

 Take the high road. Do your best to create friends and not enemies. Endeavor to end things on good terms. As one wise person said, "Never wrestle with a pig. You both get dirty, but the pig likes it."

11. Listen Well

There's a lot of noise in the world. And in spite of the fact that we have two ears and only one mouth, most people do a lot more talking than listening.

> "Be a good listener. Your ears will never get you in trouble."
> —Frank Tyger

Most people only look like they're listening, when in actuality, they're waiting for an opportunity to talk and planning what to say next.

Listening is a critical skill in the art of communication.

 Listen to others, but also listen to yourself. Listen to the inner senses of the heart. Listen to what's being said and to what's not being said. Listen without planning what you'll say next.

12. You Can't Un-ring a Bell

There's an old ditty that goes, "Sticks and stones may break my bones, but names will never hurt me." And as most of us have learned, it simply isn't so. Words can be extremely hurtful.

> "When anger rises, think of the consequences."
> —Confucius

It's true that it's our reaction to what others say that causes our pain, but we can all agree that much unnecessary distress has been caused by the utterance of unkind words. Sometimes we've been on the receiving end, and other times, we've been the one to say angry, insensitive things.

And once the words are out, you can't ever take them back. You can apologize, you can beg forgiveness, you can claim fatigue, but the damage has been done.

Obviously, the best way to avoid such conflict and harm is to simply not say thoughtless things. And it's not always easy.

Jay Leno: "You can't stay mad at somebody who makes you laugh."

Wayne Dyer: "There's nothing wrong with anger provided you use it constructively."

Whenever you're angry or upset, hold your tongue. It's never helpful to say things rashly when we're overtired, upset or angry.

Be mindful that your words—whether in person, via email or letter—can rarely be called back. You can't un-ring a bell, and you can't completely undo the damage of your angry words. So don't say them.

13. Show How Much You Care

People don't care how much you know until they know how much you care. It seems like everyone is trying to impress everyone else. But nobody really cares unless they think *you* do.

> "Those who bring sunshine to others cannot keep it from themselves."
> —Sir James Barrie

Tiger Woods: "My dad has always taught me these words: care and share. That's why we put on clinics. The only thing I can do is try to give back. If it works, it works."

Anita Roddick: "The end result of kindness is that it draws people to you."

Oprah Winfrey: "I don't think you ever stop giving. I really don't. I think it's an on-going process. And it's not just about being able to write a check. It's being able to touch somebody's life."

Barbara Bush: "To us, family means putting your arms around each other and being there."

Nelson Mandela: "If you talk to a man in a language he understands, that goes to his head. If you talk to him in his language, that goes to his heart."

The Dalai Lama: "This is my simple religion. There is no need for temples; no need for complicated philosophy. Our own brain, our own heart is our temple; the philosophy is kindness."

Instead of trying to get attention with your wit, your knowledge, your experience or your status, take a genuine interest in others. This will show you care at least a little and give you a chance to show you care a lot.

14. Be Your Word

There's probably no greater compliment that can be paid to another than something like this: "You say what you mean and you mean what you say. When you say you'll do something, I can *count* on it being done. You're a person of your word."

> "Who you are speaks so loudly, I can't hear what you say."
> —Ralph Waldo Emerson

Do people say this about *you*? Are you that kind of person? It isn't easy. And perhaps that's why it's so rare. But the payoff is substantial. Being your word goes a long way toward living a guilt-free life.

There is no such thing as a small promise. When you become casual about your agreements, you begin a pattern that's difficult to reverse. You may say to yourself, "It's OK; it's not that important." But it *is* important. Because once you start blowing off so-called small promises, you'll find it easier to shirk bigger ones.

John Maxwell reminds us: "People buy into the leader before they buy into the vision."

Norman Schwarzkopf: "Leadership is a potent combination of strategy and character. But if you must be without one, be without the strategy."

 Keep your word—not only to others, but also yourself. Don't make promises lightly. When you agree to something, keep that agreement—or renegotiate it if you're unable to do so.

 Clean the Yuck Out of Your Life!
www.SuccessNet.org/members/articles/angier-yuck.htm

15. Hang Out with the Right People

We're not talking here about only spending time with the hip and connected. We're talking about hanging out with people you trust and admire—people who support what you do and challenge you to be your best.

Your life will be the same five years from now except for the people you meet, the books you read and the tales you listen to. We all know that hanging out with mischievous people is a bad thing. But spending time with people who don't inspire us can be almost as bad.

It is difficult to say who does us the most damage, our enemies with the worst intentions or our friends with the best. A real friend is one who helps us to think our noblest thoughts, put forth our best efforts and be our best selves.

Wayne Dyer: "When you judge another, you do not define them, you define yourself."

 Choose your friends and associates carefully. You may even need to move on from some friendships. It's not that they're bad people, they just may be bad for you.

16. Marry Wisely

Choosing the person who becomes your life partner is one of—if not *the*—most important decision you will make in your lifetime. With divorce rates in North America over 50%, it's

> "I love you not for who you are, but for what I am when I am with you."
>
> —Roy Croft

apparent that, for the most part, we're not doing too well in our marital decisions.

Although it may be true that you can marry more money in five minutes than you can earn in a lifetime, don't do it. Marry for love and marry for friendship. Marry for shared values and partnership.

There's certainly risk involved. And there are no guarantees. But if you consider carefully and choose wisely, you can substantially improve your chances of a successful marriage.

Paul McCartney: "And in the end, the love you take is equal to the love you make."

 Invest the time to get clear on what you want and expect in a marriage. Talk about what you each want and expect. Ask questions. Talk about your goals and aspirations. Project yourself ahead 10, 15, 20 years . . . where do you see yourself?

17. Admit When You're Wrong

Politicians would likely become more trusted if—at least once in awhile—they admitted they were wrong. Voters don't expect perfection, but they do appreciate candid truthfulness.

> "It is common sense to take a method and try it. If it fails, admit it frankly and try another, but above all try something."
>
> —Franklin D. Roosevelt

Even if you're not a politician, be willing to be wrong. Own up to your mistakes. There's nothing wrong in making a mistake. But it's arrogant not to acknowledge it or even worse to repeat it. Too many people see the admission of mistakes as a sign of weakness rather than strength.

David Letterman: "The worst-tempered people I have ever met were those who knew that they were wrong."

 If you share your blunders, others will have more empathy for you and cut you more slack than you'd think. In doing so, you lessen the chance of repeating it yourself and may even help them to avoid the same mistake. They may even be encouraged to share their own stories.

18. Follow the Three Rules of Life

The first rule is be nice. The second rule is be nice. And the third rule is be nice.

Getting ahead in the world demands that you get along with others. Being difficult, hard to get along with, abrasive and discourteous makes your success more difficult and less enjoyable—for yourself and others.

Mary Angelou: "If you have only one smile in you, give it to the people you love. Don't be surly at home, then go out in the street and start grinning Good Morning at total strangers."

Colin Powell: "The day soldiers stop bringing you their problems is the day you have stopped leading them. They have either lost confidence that you can help them or concluded that you do not care. Either case is a failure of leadership."

 Ask a close and honest friend to review the way you act and interact with others. What do they have for suggestions to improve your "niceness factor?" Then go to work on yourself to become a nicer person.

19. Forgive Yourself and Others

An old adage goes, "If you seek revenge, dig two graves." The premise being that the harm you do to another is delivered upon you as well.

> "Since nothing we intend is ever faultless, and nothing we attempt ever without error, and nothing we achieve without some measure of finitude and fallibility we call humanness, we are saved by forgiveness."
>
> —David Augsnurger

To fully succeed, to live at your highest and best, you must not carry grudges. Learn to forgive not only other people, but also yourself for the mistakes you have and will make. In doing so, you can live in the present and move into the future instead of being run by the past.

Billy Graham: "The Christian life is not a constant high. I have my moments of deep discouragement. I have to go to God in prayer with tears in my eyes and say, 'O God, forgive me,' or 'Help me.'"

 What have you been holding onto? Who have you not forgiven? Review your life and experiences. If there's an emotional charge toward someone, you probably haven't let go. Do what you need to do in order to move forward without having to drag this heavy burden around with you.

20. Write and Send Thank You Cards

This is not and should not become a lost art. Many careers have been greatly assisted by simply taking the time to write thank you notes.

Perhaps *because* it's so infrequently done, your written messages of gratitude will stand out. In addition, it focuses you on what you've been given. The practice will help you develop an attitude of gratitude. The unexpected thank you note (and almost all of them are) is especially appreciated.

 Don't let a week go by without sending at least one thank you note.

21. Be Genuinely Interested in Others

Art Linkletter often said, "Kids say the darndest things." But it's not just kids. *People* say the most fascinating things. That is, if you're interested, if you draw them out and if you listen.

> "You can make more friends in two months by becoming interested in other people than you can in two years by trying to get other people interested in you."
>
> —Dale Carnegie

For people to be interested in *you*, be interested in others.

 Make a determined effort to pay close attention to what people are saying. Become an active listener. Instead of waiting for your turn to say something, sincerely listen and become interested in people.

 Listen, Pause, Clarify and Validate
www.SuccessNet.org/members/articles/angier-validation.htm

22. Use Written Agreements

Even when the people with whom you enter into agreement are honest and well intended, misunderstandings or lapses of memory can cause disputes.

> "With a written agreement, you have a prayer. With a verbal agreement, you have nothing but air."
>
> —unknown

It's nice to be able to do business with only a handshake, but it's hard to beat a clear, written—and *signed*—agreement. It certainly doesn't guarantee there will be no disputes, but it will surely eliminate some of the problems that a verbal agreement can create.

Tony Blair: "Now is not the time for sound-bites. I can feel the hand of history on my shoulder." (On the signing of the Good Friday Agreement)

 Always have a written agreement. Even if you enter into a verbal one, it's best to follow it with a letter of understanding, and then get a response that confirms what you've laid out in your letter.

23. Give People the Respect They Deserve

Everyone wants to be loved. But next to being loved, they want to be respected. You can never err by being respectful to the people you encounter. It matters not what position someone has or their social status. Everyone is a human being and deserves to be treated respectfully.

Kofi Annan wrote: "We may have different religions, different languages, different colored skin, but we all belong to one human race."

Tom Peters: "The magic formula that successful businesses have discovered is to treat customers like guests and employees like people."

Robert Schuller: "As we grow as unique persons, we learn to respect the uniqueness of others."

Oprah Winfrey: "You cannot hate other people without hating yourself."

 Be courteous. Be considerate. Call people by their name. Act and speak in a respectful fashion to everyone you come into contact with. You don't have to agree with everyone, but you can—and should—respect them.

MOTIVATION

All success requires a desire to achieve. Getting motivated, staying motivated and motivating others is an important part of getting ahead in the world. The following represents solid gold counsel for doing just that.

24. Clarity Leads to Power

Motivation is simply a strong desire to move toward something you want or away from something you don't want. How motivated we are depends largely upon how much we want or *don't* want something.

One of the biggest challenges facing people and companies is lack of clarity about what they want and why they want it. Once we're clear, once we have a big enough why, there's really no stopping us.

> "I always wanted to be somebody, but I should have been more specific."
>
> —Lily Tomlin

> "Clarity of mind means clarity of passion, too; this is why a great and clear mind loves ardently and sees distinctly what it loves."
>
> —Blaise Pascal

It is the clarity that leads to power.

Brian Tracy: "The greater clarity you have with regard to your future vision for yourself, and your current goals, the easier it will be for you to make decisions, the more you will be motivated to carry out those decisions and the more determined you will become to succeed."

Edward de Bono: "An expert is someone who has succeeded in making decisions and judgments simpler through knowing what to pay attention to and what to ignore."

 If you find yourself not making the progress you'd like to make, take a look at what it is you're really going for—and why? Can you clearly articulate it to someone else? Do they get it? Can you see it? Can you feel it? Does it excite you?

 The Principle of Vacuum
www.SuccessNet.org/articles/angier-vacuum.htm

25. Set Lofty Goals

Big goals motivate. Small goals rarely do. A big goal provides the juice, the power and the drive to move you forward and overcome the obstacles that will surely come your way.

> "When we realize one Dream, sometimes a deeper Dream reveals itself. At other times a parallel Dream appears. The one that scares the hell out of you is probably it."
>
> —Peter McWilliams

A goal that will eventually become accomplished without much effort on your part is more likely an *event* rather than a goal. They are OK to have, but to really grow, you need goals that make you stretch. They need to be believable—at least to you—but they should be enough of a stretch that it scares you just a little.

Mark Victor Hansen: "Big goals get big results. No goals get no results—or somebody else's results."

Zig Ziglar reminds us: "What you get by achieving your goals is not as important as what you become by achieving your goals."

Anthony Robbins: "Setting goals is the first step in turning the invisible into the visible."

 What are your goals? Which ones are the big ones—maybe even the ones you haven't quite dared to articulate? Maybe that's what's missing—a big, hairy, audacious goal. Think big.

26. Be Decisive

Too many dreams have been left unrealized and too many great things have been left undone because someone was unwilling to make a decision. They held back. They procrastinated. They waited for additional information and better advice. But in hesitating, they either lost their momentum or never created any to start with.

> "Indecision is debilitating; it feeds upon itself; it is, one might almost say, habit-forming. Not only that, but it is contagious; it transmits itself to others."
>
> —H.A. Hopf

In an ideal world, you could have all the experience and all the information you need to make the best decision. But as General Patton said, "An imperfect plan executed today is better then a perfect plan tomorrow."

Deepak Chopra: "You and I are essentially infinite choice-makers. In every moment of our existence, we are in that field of all possibilities where we have access to an infinity of choices."

Margaret Thatcher: "I usually make up my mind about a man in ten seconds; and I very rarely change it."

Michael Dell: "We cannot do everything at once. We have to prioritize which opportunities are best for us and for our customers."

Lee Iacocca: "If I had to sum up in one word what makes a good manager, I'd say decisiveness. You can use the fanciest computers to gather the numbers, but in the end you have to set a timetable and act."

Tony Blair: "The art of leadership is saying no, not yes. It is very easy to say yes."

 Be willing to make decisions without being absolutely certain. Successful people make decisions quickly and change them slowly, if at all.

27. You Have to Believe

In order to really be motivated, you have to be clear on your objectives, but you also have to believe you can achieve them. It's rare that anyone accomplishes anything that deep down inside they didn't *believe* they could.

Arnold Schwarzenegger knows it well: "The mind is the limit. As long as the mind can envision the fact that you can do something, you can do it, as long as you really believe 100 percent."

Billy Graham: "Courage is contagious. When a brave man takes a stand, the spines of others are often stiffened."
Barbra Streisand: "You have got to discover you, what you do, and trust it."

 What do you *really* believe you're capable of achieving? What do you *say* you believe, but actually don't? Be honest. Look for the areas in which you need to shore up your belief and confidence. Then, find ways to increase your belief. For instance, find someone who's already done it.

28. Tough Times Never Last but Tough People Do

That's Dr. Robert Schuller talking. We all experience setbacks and disappointments. Everyone gets discouraged. The danger is that we think we've been singled out—and that other so-called successful people don't experience these frustrations.

Our lives include many cycles. Some times are easy and some times are hard. It's valuable to remember the hard times when things are easy and the easy times when things are hard.

Zig Ziglar says, "Failure is a detour, not a dead-end street."

Nelson Mandela: "There is no easy walk to freedom anywhere, and many of us will have to pass through the valley of the shadow of death again and again before we reach the mountaintop of our desires."

Andre Agassi: "What makes something special is not just what you have to gain, but what you feel there is to lose."

Ted Turner: "You can never quit. Winners never quit, and quitters never win."

Be a person who can weather the storms. Remember that what doesn't kill us makes us stronger. Decide to endure your challenges, and know that you will emerge a better and stronger person.

MONEY/FINANCE

Interestingly enough, not much advice was offered from our "101 Most Successful" about money or finance. Do they think so little of money because most of them have so much of it? Or do they have so much of it because they think so little about it?

Bob Proctor has this to say about money: "Money is an idea. The paper you fold and place in your purse or pocket is not money. It is paper with ink on it. It *represents* money, but it is not money. Money is an idea. The earning of money has nothing to do with the paper stuff. It has to do with consciousness."

29. Pay Yourself First

Financial advisors agree. In order to develop good savings and a dependable retirement portfolio, you have to pay yourself first. Anyone, that's right, *anyone*—even someone making a meager wage—can become a millionaire by saving as little as 10% of their income and making compound interest work to their advantage. If you start early enough, it's virtually guaranteed.

So why doesn't everyone do this?

It's simply a matter of discipline. It's not all that hard, but it does require a commitment to save regularly. Consistency and longevity is the key in building a large portfolio.

The earlier you start, of course, the easier it will be to grow a large retirement. Even someone earning a modest wage can become a millionaire if they start early and make deposits each and every pay period.

 Regardless of how old or young you are, start today. Put something away every week. The progress may seem slow at first, but like a snowball rolling downhill, it will continue to grow and pick up speed. Pay yourself first. No matter what your age, start today and contribute consistently to an IRA.

30. Track Your Finances

You can't change what you don't measure. People who aren't doing well financially usually don't have a very good handle on the money coming in and the money going out. They convince themselves that when they have *more* money, they will have better accounting.

But that's not the way it works. You have to master the small things in order to graduate to the larger things. And no place is this more evident than in financial accounting.

Warren Buffet: "In the business world, the rearview mirror is always clearer than the windshield."

Use a good accounting software like MS Money® or Quicken® for your personal finances. QuickBooks® is great for business accounting. Know where you are. Know where you've been. And know where you're going by easily tracking it all using these tools. You'll stay on top of your finances and make significant progress.

Metrics Make a Difference—And Money, Too
www.SuccessNet.org/members/articles/angier-metrics.htm

31. Borrow for Assets—not Liabilities

Assets appreciate. Liabilities demand payment and/or cost money to maintain—either now or in the future.

> "'Tis against some men's principle to pay interest, and seems against other's interest to pay the principle."
>
> —Benjamin Franklin

When you borrow for things that depreciate or have no initial resale value, you're not using credit to your best advantage. A vacation, entertainment or consumables are hardly ever a good thing to buy on credit.

Borrowing for things that *do* appreciate is an investment. Real estate and tools to run your business are worthy of going into debt. Some would argue that a debt backed up by a saleable asset of equal or greater value shouldn't even be called debt.

Borrow wisely. Do your best to borrow only when you're able to show a corresponding asset to offset the debt. In doing so, you will be moving your net worth upward rather than downward.

32. Profits are Better than Wages

Almost everyone in the world sells their time. The problem is, there's only a certain amount of it to sell. By increasing our value—upgrading our skills, specializing, increasing our knowledge and experience—we can earn more per hour, per day or per month. But the limitation of the number of hours in the day and weeks in the year create a cap on what we can earn.

More and more, we have an opportunity to get paid based upon what value we create—what something's *worth* rather than for what we do.

But there's no cap on what you can make with the profits from a company. The tax laws in most developing countries are written in favor of free enterprise because lawmakers know that this is how economies are driven.

Robert Schuller: "Our greatest lack is not money for any undertaking, but rather ideas. If the ideas are good, cash will somehow flow to where it is needed."

 In what ways do you earn income from profits as opposed to wages? How can you create a desirable service or product that will allow you to earn profits? What needs are not yet being met? What new trends can you use to your advantage?

33. Getting Wealthy

Robert Allen believes, " . . . in the whole wide world of money there are only four ways of becoming a millionaire . . . 1. investments, 2. real estate, 3. business, 4. internet."

We questioned that a little bit, but really can't think of much else.

Bill Gates: "The internet will help achieve 'friction free capitalism' by putting buyer and seller in direct contact and providing more information to both about each other."

 Which one(s) of these four will you invest your time, energy and resources?

34. Your Self Worth Affects Your Net Worth

Part of developing a consciousness of abundance is learning to appreciate and value people and things. As you enhance your self worth, you perceive yourself as more worthy of wealth in its many forms.

You are a child of God and are worthy of all God's blessings. You have a purpose and you have unique value.

Jim Rohn: "Money is usually attracted, not pursued."

Focus on your attributes and your value as a person. Pay little attention, if any, to your shortcomings.

35. Make Money While You Sleep

Passive income—or what some call residual income—is income that does not require your direct involvement. Real estate, licensing, product invention, royalties and your investment portfolio are all examples of things that can provide passive income for you.

It doesn't matter whether you're self-employed or work for someone else—there are many ways you can create and develop income streams that don't require your presence.

The trick is to have money working for you instead you working for the money.

Time is a finite and fleeting resource. Having passive income streams, on the other hand, is like owning oil wells that continue to pump and profit—while you do other things.

Robert Kiyosaki: "The difference between a rich person and poor person is how they use their time."

Jim Rohn: "To become financially independent, you must turn part of your income into capital; turn capital into enterprise; turn enterprise into profit; turn profit into investment; and turn investment into financial independence."

 Brainstorm ways you can create or enhance income streams that flow without your constant effort and attention. Pick one or two, and go to work on them. It's a worthy investment of your time and pays big—and long-lasting—dividends.

CREATIVITY

Creativity plays a large role in moving us forward, navigating change and accomplishing our goals. One of the greatest thinkers of the last century, Albert Einstein, wrote, "All meaningful and lasting change starts first in your imagination and then works its way out. Imagination is more important than knowledge."

Successful people know this and tap into their creativity to achieve their objectives. Here are several succinct ideas to help you achieve yours.

36. Innovation: Ideas are Cheap but Extremely Valuable

At the turn of the last century, there was serious discussion about disbanding the U.S. Patent Office because many believed there were few inventions left to be patented. The common wisdom was that all the great inventions had already been created. No doubt there are people today who feel the same way.

> "Ideas not coupled with action never become bigger than the brain cells they occupied."
>
> —Arnold Glasgow
>
> "Getting an idea should be like sitting on a pin: it should make you jump up and do something."
>
> —E. L. Simpson

The world is entering a time of unprecedented innovation. We're experiencing some of the greatest prosperity we've ever known. Productivity is at an all-time high. And when basic needs are met, it's easier to be creative.

Innovation is not only for so-called "creative" minds. We're all creative, and each of us has the ability to generate ideas to solve problems in our businesses and improve our relationships.

Innovation is nothing more than taking information and reorganizing it in new ways.

It's important to take some of our increased productivity and use some of the time saved to think and create. Ask questions. Dig deep. Think about what you want and what others might want. What problems need to be solved, and how can we solve them? Remember that it's okay to borrow ideas, as long as you don't borrow them all from one place.

Ideas are cheap. It's implementation that creates the real value. Ideas by themselves are worthless. Plans are nothing . . . unless they are followed with action. An idea without a strategy, without action, is useless.

Edward de Bono: "Creativity is a great motivator because it makes people interested in what they are doing. Creativity gives hope that there can be a worthwhile idea. Creativity gives the possibility of some sort of achievement to everyone. Creativity makes life more fun and more interesting."

Meg Whitman: "You can kill a man, but you can't kill an idea."

 It's paramount we keep track of the ideas we have. Write them down. Record them in some fashion. And make them easy to access later. You never know when an idea may trigger another one that could be just the one to make you a million dollars—or save a million. Make sure you record it somewhere. If you make it easy to do, you'll do more of it.

Use your Task List in Microsoft Outlook® to keep track of ideas. You can categorize them and make them easy to find. Index cards also work well. They fit handily in a shirt pocket or purse and are easy to sort and categorize. You can even use your journal or a separate document on your word processor. The easier it is to find and review them, the more valuable your ideas will be to you.

Pick the best, implement them and watch your life—and even the lives of those around you—work better.

37. Don't Think it, Ink it

Keep a journal. Life happens very quickly and when you write in a journal, it helps you to slow things down and enables you to reflect upon what happens, what you learn and what you experience. As you write, you create more clarity and enrich your life.

Mark Victor Hansen: "You control your future, your destiny. What you think about comes about. By recording your dreams and goals on paper, you set in motion the process of becoming the person you most want to be. Put your future in good hands—your own."

 Begin keeping a journal and commit to writing in it regularly. You'll be amazed at the value you'll receive by reviewing your entries weeks, months and years later. A good tool for an electronic journal is Microsoft OneNote®.

38. Completions

Things we complete provide us with space to be more creative. When we're faced with lists of things that remain undone or incomplete, it siphons off much of our energy and creativity.

> "The future belongs to those who believe in the beauty of their dreams."
> —Eleanor Roosevelt

And when we complete something, we feel a sense of accomplishment. It releases endorphins that give us a small high. On the other hand, when we're faced with lots of things undone, we often feel guilty, stressed and overwhelmed.

Jack Welch: "Good business leaders create a vision, articulate the vision, passionately own the vision, and relentlessly drive it to completion."

 What can you complete today? Take one thing and get it done, out of sight and out of mind. Try to complete *something* every day. This will get you in the habit of finishing things.

39. Take a Different Route

Problems are rarely solved on the same level they are created. Thinking outside the box is a common recommendation. Sometimes we even need to create a new box.

If what you're doing isn't working, it's usually time to do something different. What should you be doing differently? Well, anything is better than what you're doing, if what you're doing is ineffective.

Edward de Bono: "It is better to have enough ideas for some of them to be wrong, than to be always right by having no ideas at all."

Steve Jobs: "You can't just ask customers what they want and then try to give that to them. By the time you get it built, they'll want something new."

 Look for a different path. Or create a new one. There are an infinite number of possibilities.

40. Put Your House in Order

When you clear the clutter from your life, you'll find yourself able to be more creative. Clutter and chaos block the creative flow and extinguish the creative spark.

Having good systems and operating in an organized environment frees your mind to think more clearly and be more creative.

 Look for areas of your life that are messy. Clear out, clean up and organize your physical environment. And start somewhere today.

41. Problems are Opportunities

If you can begin to see all problems as possible opportunities, you'll not only solve more problems, you'll stretch, grow and become stronger. You will become known as the person who can "get it done."

Michael Jordan: "Always turn a negative situation into a positive situation."

Lee Iacocca: "We are continually faced with great opportunities brilliantly disguised as insoluble problems."

Edward de Bono: "Sometimes the situation is only a problem because it is looked at in a certain way. Looked at in another way, the right course of action may be so obvious that the problem no longer exists."

Robert Schuller: "Again and again, the impossible problem is solved when we see that the problem is only a tough decision waiting to be made."

Lee Iacocca: "We are continually faced by great opportunities brilliantly disguised as insoluble problems."

Tom Cruise: "When you have to cope with a lot of problems, you're either going to sink or you're going to swim."

 With every problem you face, look for what it may present as an opportunity. Never lament your situation—look for the lemonade you can make from your lemons.

42. Take Time to Moodle

It's important to be productive. But you also have to allow for what we call moodling time—down time used for thinking, daydreaming and lazing about. It's during these times that we're often struck with the blinding flash of the obvious. It's when we can tap into our imagination.

Muhammad Ali: "The man who has no imagination has no wings."

Steven Spielberg: "I dream for a living."

J.K. Rowling: "Always have a vivid imagination, for you never know when you might need it."

Gloria Steinem: "Without leaps of imagination, or dreaming, we lose the excitement of possibilities. Dreaming, after all, is a form of planning."

 Vacation is not the only time to take time off. It just happens to be a time of *extended* time off. Make room in your schedule to do nothing at all—and then do it.

43. Get Comfortable Being Uncomfortable

Great things are never accomplished easily. Too many people spend their energies attempting to remain in their comfort zone. In doing so, they forfeit their grandest dreams and highest aspirations. And they deprive themselves of the growth and learning that comes from stretching and broadening their experiences.

> "Be willing to be uncomfortable. Be comfortable being uncomfortable. It may get tough, but it's a small price to pay for living a dream."
> —Peter McWilliams

The vast majority of people are trying to avoid the uncomfortable. Achievers know that they'll gain the most success by doing things that are goal achieving instead of tension relieving.

Billy Graham: "Comfort and prosperity have never enriched the world as much as adversity."

 Resolve to stretch yourself by doing the uncomfortable. In doing so, you will increase your ability and willingness to do the things that will move you forward and achieve your goals.

MISSION/VISION

Muhammad Ali may have said it best: "Champions aren't made in gyms. Champions are made from something they have deep inside them: A desire, a dream, a vision. They have to have last-minute stamina, they have to be a little faster, they have to have the skill and the will. But the will must be stronger than the skill."

44. Think Big

It costs nothing to think big. Almost all of our "101 Most Successful" thought bigger than most others. They didn't think they were really any better or more entitled than others. They simply followed their hearts and trusted that God wouldn't have given them a big dream without the means to accomplish it.

Donald Trump wrote, "As long as you're going to be thinking anyway, you might as well think big."

Small dreams don't inspire. Big dreams do. Gloria Steinem wrote, "If what's in your dreams wasn't already real inside you, you couldn't even dream it."

Barbara Bush: "Believe in something larger than yourself. . . Get involved in the big ideas of your time."

Mikhail Gorbachev: "If what you have done yesterday still looks big to you, you haven't done much today."

Bill Clinton: "Big things are expected of us, and nothing big ever came of being small."

 Dream big. Read stories of great accomplishments. Hang out with people who will encourage you to live high on the go-for-it scale.

45. Have a Purpose

Buckminster Fuller once said, "Your true purpose will forever remain obscure." But he was speaking metaphysically. You really can

> "The purpose of life is a life of purpose."
>
> —Robert Byrne

determine what your purpose is and live that purpose.

Having a purpose provides more meaning and a greater sense of satisfaction. It makes your decisions easier and enables you to live with more satisfaction and fulfillment.

Cheryl Richardson: "Turn your life into a work of art, and let your soul show you where you need to go."

Pope John Paul II: "When freedom does not have a purpose, when it does not wish to know anything about the rule of law engraved in the hearts of men and women, when it does not listen to the voice of conscience, it turns against humanity and society."

Bob Proctor: "Your *purpose* explains *what* you are doing with your life. Your *vision* explains how you are living your *purpose*. Your *goals* enable you to realize your *vision*."

John McCain: "Glory is not a conceit. It is not a decoration for valor. Glory belongs to the act of being constant to something greater than yourself, to a cause, to your principles, to the people on whom you rely and who rely on you in return.

 Invest the time to explore and discover your true purpose. You find what you're looking for so *look* for it. You absolutely do have one. Then, orient your life around that purpose. Otherwise you'll always feel frustrated and off-balance.

46. If You Don't Ask, You Don't Get

Getting ahead in the world demands that you become a good asker—not a good suggester, not a good hoper, not a good beggar—a good *asker*.

Successful people have mastered the art of asking. They ask for what they want. They ask for what they can do in return. They ask for what's needed. Are *you* good at asking?

Jim Rohn: "Asking is the beginning of receiving. Make sure you don't go to the ocean with a teaspoon. At least take a bucket so the kids won't laugh at you."

 Ask for what you want. Ask clearly. Ask with expectation. Ask often. Ask someone who can help. Ask until.

47. Don't Let Anyone Steal Your Dream

Our fondest dreams and highest aspirations may very well be our most valuable possessions. And yet we don't protect them nearly as well as we do our material assets.

> "Keep away from people who try to belittle your ambitions. Small people always do that, but the really great make you feel that you, too, can become great."
>
> —Mark Twain

And unlike material possessions, our dreams are often stolen by those people who are closest to us. Sometimes well-intended, but misdirected friends and relatives, can do us the greatest harm—by pouring cold water on our hopes and dreams.

We must safeguard our ambitions. It is critical we guard them from the dream killers and spirit suckers. It is easy for people to ridicule, disparage and criticize our goals and abilities. Some engage in it almost like it was a sport.

Try looking at the "advice" from the dream stealers as a test of how serious you are about going for your big goals.

Our dreams need tender care and nourishment—especially in the early stages. Nurture them well.

Jim Rohn advises: "If you don't design your own life plan, chances are you'll fall into someone else's plan. And guess what they have planned for you. Not much."

Bill Clinton: "Success is not the measure of a man but a triumph over those who choose to hold him back."

 Share your big goals and dreams only with people you know who will be supportive. Don't listen to the naysayers. Stay around people who will be honest about your plans but who encourage rather than discourage you.

And remember what Frank Sinatra said, "The best revenge is massive success."

48. Questions are the Answers

A good coach or consultant asks good questions. A good therapist asks good questions. The value they provide is not so much the advice they give but rather the clarity they help the business manager or the patient achieve.

Elegant questions make you think. Good questions uncover what is not so evident on the surface. Good questions help you solve problems and make better decisions.

Poor questions are questions like: Why is this happening to me? What have I done wrong to deserve this? Why can't I ever learn? These kind of questions lead nowhere and are even counterproductive.

Brian Tracy: "A major stimulant to creative thinking is focused questions. There is something about a well-worded question that often penetrates to the heart of the matter and triggers new ideas and insights."

Anthony Robbins: "Quality questions create a quality life. Successful people ask better questions, and as a result, they get better answers."

To think more clearly and gain the many benefits outlined above, develop the skill of asking and thinking through elegant questions.

Laser Questions™—a system for helping you generate solutions to problems.
www.SuccessNet.org/laserq.htm

49. Become and Remain Focused

Many great opportunities have been squandered because focus has been scattered. No one and no company can be master of everything. There's no way to focus on everything at once.

Staying on track day in and day out is what it takes to weave successful days into a successful life.

Anthony Robbins: "One reason so few of us achieve what we truly want is

> "If a man is called to be a street sweeper, he should sweep streets even as Michelangelo painted or Beethoven played music, or Shakespeare wrote poetry. He should sweep streets so well that all the hosts of heaven and earth will pause to say, here lived a great street sweeper who did his job well."
>
> —Martin Luther King, Jr.

that we never direct our focus; we never concentrate our power. Most people dabble their way through life, never deciding to master anything in particular."

Meg Whitman: "A business leader has to keep their organization focused on the mission. That sounds easy, but it can be tremendously challenging in today's competitive and ever-changing business environment. A leader also has to motivate potential partners to join the cause."

Tiger Woods: "I am the toughest golfer mentally."

Oprah Winfrey: "I knew there was a way out. I knew there was another kind of life because I had read about it. I knew there were other places, and there was another way of being."

 Become clear on your values. Stay clear on your mission and your goals. Then, pick the objectives and the projects that will have the greatest impact on your mission. The more focused you are, the more successful you'll be.

 The Top Ten Ways to Stay Focused on Your Objectives
www.SuccessNet.org/topten/TTfocused.htm

HEALTH

Good health is the first wealth. Without it, all our other successes have little value. Becoming and/or remaining healthy should be a critical objective and worthy of our best efforts. Understand these concepts and follow these practices for good health.

50. A Positive Mental Attitude

So much of success has to do with attitude. It takes optimism to achieve exceptional results.

> "A happy person is not a person in a certain set of circumstances, but rather a person with a certain set of attitudes."
>
> —Hugh Downs

Norman Vincent Peale said it well when he wrote, "Any fact facing us is not as important as our attitude toward it, for that determines our success or failure. The way you think about a fact may defeat you before you ever do anything about it. You are overcome by the fact because you think you are."

Arnold Schwarzenegger: "Strength does not come from winning. Your struggles develop your strengths. When you go through hardships and decide not to surrender, that is strength."

John Maxwell: "Failure is not fatal. Only the failure to get back up."

 Attitude is a choice. So choose to be positive. Look for the good in things. Follow the advice of Michael Jordan, "Always turn a negative situation into a positive situation."

51. Get Plenty of Rest

Many scientists agree that most westerners go through their lives suffering from sleep deprivation. In the 24/7 world in which we live, routines and adequate sleep often go by the wayside.

Don't let this happen to you. Vince Lombard said, "Fatigue makes cowards of us all." To have the courage, the stamina and the clear thinking it takes to get ahead in the world, you need to get sufficient sleep. You need breaks. You need vacations.

 Get the rest you need. Understand your energy patterns and make them work to your advantage. Give yourself permission to get the sleep you need and then *sleep*.

52. Be Gentle with Yourself

To really move ahead in the world, we need to challenge ourselves to be our best. But we *also* need to be gentle with ourselves.

No one is perfect. Everyone—at least those *doing* anything—makes mistakes. We need to be able to forgive ourselves and move one. We call it "correction without invalidation."

All too often people blame themselves instead of their actions. They're unable to make the distinction between the actions and the one doing the acting.

Phil McGraw: "Life is a marathon; it's not a sprint."

Cheryl Richardson: "True success comes from the amount of time you spend at peace with yourselves and with loved ones. Fame and fortune really don't mean anything at all."

Stephen Covey: "Be patient with yourself. Self-growth is tender; it's holy ground. There's no greater investment."

 Spend no time attending pity parties. What's done is done. Learn and move on. It is the only way to make significant progress.

53. Don't Take Yourself Too Seriously

It's true that some people don't take themselves or their lives seriously enough. But many people take themselves *way* too seriously. It's best to develop the ability to laugh at yourself. In doing so, you'll enjoy better health and be a lot easier to be around.

Early in his ministry, the Reverend Billy Graham once stopped in a small town where he was scheduled to preach. Wanting to mail a letter, he asked a young boy where the post office was. After the boy provided directions, Dr. Graham thanked him and then invited the boy to the Baptist church where he would be telling people how to get to heaven. "I don't think I'll be there," the boy said. "You don't even know how to get to the post office."

 Things are rarely as serious as they seem at the time. Almost all of the things you think are a big deal now are things you'll chuckle about later. So if you're going to laugh about it later, you might as well laugh about it now. And remember, don't sweat the small stuff—and it's almost all small stuff.

54. Live with Passion

Not only should you *find* your passion (as in your calling), but you should live with passion. Enthusiasm is contagious. And *not* having enthusiasm is also contagious. A

> "Catch on fire with enthusiasm and people will come for miles to watch you burn."
>
> —John Wesley

powerful enthusiasm affects everyone around you. People are attracted to, will work hard for and enjoy being around people who are excited.

Nothing great has ever been accomplished without enthusiasm. We don't know the source of this quote, but we like what it says: "Work like you don't need the money. Love like you've never been hurt. Dance like nobody's watching, and pray like the answer's already on the way."

Robin Williams: "You're only given a little spark of madness. You mustn't lose it."

Stephen King: "Get busy living, or get busy dying."

 Do things with verve. Have at least as much excitement for what you're doing as you do for your favorite sports team.

55. Maintain a Sense of Humor

Studies prove that a good sense of humor enhances your health. A good belly laugh can cure all kinds of ailments.

> "Catch on fire with enthusiasm and people will come for miles to watch you burn."
>
> —John Wesley
>
> "Laughter is the shortest distance between two people."
>
> —Victor Borge

Jim Rohn: "You can be serious about what you're doing without being grim." Some people—especially in business settings—hold back on their humor for fear of being judged less than serious. In fact, a good sense of humor is admired in the business world. Your skills, knowledge and experience are more marketable if they come wrapped with good humor.

Stephen King: "You can't deny laughter; when it comes, it plops down in your favorite chair and stays as long as it wants."

 Be sure to laugh often. Look for the humor in every situation. Never be ashamed to laugh.

56. Producer vs. Production

Stephen Covey talks about production vs. production capacity. We place a lot of emphasis on our production, but Covey's point is that we must pay attention to our production *capacity*. If our production is our golden eggs, then we are the goose that lays those golden eggs. It's much more important to take excellent care of the goose than the eggs.

You can't be of much service to yourself or anyone else and you can't make much progress in this world if your production capacity is lacking. If you're sick, hurt, overtired or unhealthy, your ability to succeed is proportionately reduced.

 Take excellent care of yourself. Service to others—which is the only way to create value in the world—demands that you be healthy, safe, fresh and alert. You know how to do it. So do it.

57. Spend on the Inside as Well as the Outside

Vast sums of money are spent on clothes, cosmetics, haircuts, jewelry and more. But we also have to invest on the inside as well as the outside. This means good, healthy, nutritious food. It means taking care of yourself in terms of reducing stress and enhancing serenity.

 Be sure to invest on the inside of your body. Get a massage. Find ways to pamper yourself and rejuvenate your spirit. Take time off. Go to places you find relaxing, inspiring and refreshing. Eat good, healthy foods.

VALUES

Stephen Covey: "There is no shortcut. But there is a path. The path is based on principles revered throughout history. If there is one message to glean from this wisdom, it is that a meaningful life is not a matter of speed or efficiency. It's much more a matter of what you do and why you do it than how fast you get it done."

58. Know Your Core Values

Sound core values are the foundation of a truly successful life.

Without clear and meaningful values, any success you achieve is short-lived or unfulfilling—perhaps both.

In order for you to create excellence, there must be a strong foundation for you to build upon. Build that foundation with solid values and a strong sense of purpose, and your results are nothing short of magical.

By knowing who you are, what you believe and what you stand for, you'll make better and quicker decisions.

Rudy Giuliani: "There are many qualities that make a great leader. But having strong beliefs, being able to stick with them through popular and unpopular times, is the most important characteristic of a great leader."

Invest the time to discover, develop and detail your core values.

Your Core Values eCourse
www.YourCoreValues.com

59. Authenticity

Winston Churchill once said, "The people cannot look up to a leader who has his ear to the ground." Leaders, by definition, should *lead* not follow.

> "We need to find the courage to say NO to the things and people that are not serving us if we want to rediscover ourselves and live our lives with authenticity."
>
> — Barbara De Angelis

Originality and individuality are two of the hallmarks of true leadership. You don't have to agree with someone in order to respect them as a leader. If they feel strongly about something, and you get that they truly believe in what they're saying, you'll at least listen and consider what they have to say.

When someone's telling the truth—speaking from the heart with strong feeling—it's almost impossible to be bored.

There's a Bible phrase that we've found easy to remember: "Be hot or cold, but if you be lukewarm, I will spew thee out of my mouth."

Strong words, indeed. What we get from it is, be one way or the other. Being middle-of-the-road doesn't work. The one who has an original approach has the makings of a leader.

When we mouth the words of someone else or speak what we think others want to hear, we relinquish our power. When we speak from the heart with strong feeling and our own thinking, we stand out from the crowd.

The word "original" comes from the root word origin. And origin is the thing from which anything comes, the starting point or source. Thus, cultivating our originality is only a matter of going back to whence we came—our spirit or God-force.

We may all come from the same source, but we all express our originality in different ways. It's up to us to discover our own uniqueness—or own inner splendor. Only in doing so will we actualize our true potential and affect our purpose in the world.

Margaret Thatcher: "Being powerful is like being a lady. If you have to tell people you are, you aren't."

 Resolve to be yourself. After all, no one is better qualified. You were born an original; don't die a copy.

 Is Your Company the Real McCoy?
www.SuccessNet.org/articles/angier-realmccoy.htm

The Top Ten Reasons to Live a Life of Integrity
www.SuccessNet.org/topten/TTintegrity.htm

60. Don't Settle for Less than You Deserve

When you settle, you're telling yourself you're not worth it. You're affirming a belief in lack instead of abundance. You're saying you don't believe in yourself enough to have what you really want.

To get ahead in the world, you have to value yourself. If you don't value yourself, who else will?

Jim Rohn: "If you are not willing to risk the unusual, you will have to settle for the ordinary."

Anthony Robbins: "We can change our lives. We can do, have and be exactly what we wish."

 Be careful you don't begin to settle for less than you truly want.

 Get What You Want
www.SuccessNet.org/articles/angier-getwhatyouwant.htm

"*A Different Approach to Goal Setting: What Do You Really Want.*"
To receive this tool at no cost (in MS Word format), send an email to desire@SuccessNet.org

61. Be True to Yourself

Shakespeare's admonition to Polonius has become a cliché. But it's still sound advice: "To thine own self be true. And it shall follow as the night the day, thou canst be false to any man."

It takes less energy to be yourself. Putting on airs, trying to be someone you're not, requires too much energy and a far better memory than most of us have. We're all for being the best you can be, but make sure it's still *you*. There's real comfort and satisfaction in being yourself.

Kofi Annan wrote, "To live is to choose. But to choose well, you must know who you are and what you stand for, where you want to go and why you want to get there."

And Cheryl Richardson: "True success comes from the amount of time you spend at peace with yourself and with loved ones. Fame and fortune really don't mean anything at all."

J.K. Rowling: "It is our choices that show what we truly are, far more than our abilities."

 Invest the time to discover and understand who you are, what you want and what you're willing to stand for. It's not enough to tell the truth to others; you have to tell *yourself* the truth. In doing so, you build a life of integrity.

62. Be Responsible

Mayor Rudy Giuliani has a two-word sign on his desk that says, "I'm Responsible." And he lives by it.

He does his best to be fully accountable for what he does and what he fails to do.

Unfortunately, people who take full responsibility for themselves are the exception rather than the rule. Today, too many people refuse to take responsibility for themselves and, instead, sue others, not because they were negligent, but because they simply have deep pockets. And all of us pay for this in higher insurance premiums and added service costs.

Taking responsibility is not just the right thing to do, it's a practical and effective thing to do. When you explain away your actions and make excuses, you weaken yourself—in your own estimation and in the eyes of others. People don't expect you to be perfect; they *do* want you to be responsible.

If you really want to do something, you'll find a way. And if you don't, you'll find an excuse.

Norman Schwarzkopf: "The truth of the matter is that you always know the right thing to do. The hard part is doing it."

Tony Robbins: "I believe life is constantly testing us for our level of commitment, and life's greatest rewards are reserved for those who demonstrate a never-ending commitment to act until they achieve. This level of resolve can move mountains, but it must be constant and consistent. As simplistic as this may sound, it is still the common denominator separating those who live their dreams from those who live in regret."

Oprah Winfrey: "My philosophy is that not only are you responsible for your life, but doing the best at this moment puts you in the best place for the next moment."

 Resolve to be responsible. Don't complain or explain. Instead, take responsibility. Be accountable, and you'll stand head and shoulders above the masses.

63. Have a Vision

Phil McGraw: "Champions get what they want because they know what they want. They have a vision that keeps them motivated and efficiently on track. They see it, feel it and experience it in their minds and hearts."

You must define your own success. No one else can do that—unless you let them.

John Maxwell cautions, however: "People buy into the leader before they buy into the vision."

 Visualize what you want. Hear it. Feel it. Experience it ahead of time to make it real and make sure you want it. In doing so, you'll begin to create your vision.

64. Succeed by Helping Others

Zig Ziglar says, "You can get whatever you want in life if you only help enough others get what *they* want." It's the age-old biblical wisdom: You have to give in order to receive.

Your efforts to help others will not go unnoticed or unrewarded.

Brian Tracy: "Successful people are always looking for opportunities to help others. Unsuccessful people are always asking, 'What's in it for me?'"

> "Consciously or unconsciously, every one of us does render some service or other. If we cultivate the habit of doing this service deliberately, our desire for service will steadily grow stronger and we will make not only our own happiness, but that of the world at large."
> —Mahatma Gandhi

Norman Schwarzkopf: "You can't help someone get up a hill without getting closer to the top yourself."

 What is the service you can best render to help others succeed? Instead of focusing on what you're going to *get*, focus on what you're going to *give*.

INDUSTRY/PRODUCTIVITY

By its very definition, all success requires action. Getting things done effectively, efficiently and consistently plays a critical role in how we get along in the world. Persistence rules. Dozens of our "101 Most Successful" are wonderful examples of success through persistence. They owe their achievements to dogged determination. The following ideas, action points and resources will help you get more of the right things done.

65. Persist Until You Succeed

Brian Tracy probably articulated this better than anyone. "Resolve in advance that you will persist until you succeed. The ability to persist in the face of disappointment and defeat is the critical character quality that is indispensable to success."

An interviewer once asked Lance Armstrong, "Who or what was your primary focus during your battle with cancer?" His answer: "Easy. I was only focused on living." To get ahead, you have to stay in the game.

Ted Turner: "You can never quit. Winners never quit, and quitters never win."

And Colin Powell: "There are no secrets to success. It is the result of preparation, hard work and learning from failure."

Maya Angelou: "We may encounter many defeats, but we must not be defeated."

 Be the person who persists until they succeed. Don't give up when things become difficult. That's usually a sign that you're almost there. Make a decision well before you face the inevitable obstacles and difficulties of life that no matter what happens, you will never give up.

66. Actions Speak Louder than Words

Ross Perot said it well when he said, "Talk is cheap, words are plentiful, deeds are precious." And Eddie Guest wrote, "I would rather see a sermon than hear one any day." Both men are saying the same thing.

> "The great end of life is not knowledge but action."
>
> —Thomas Henry Huxley
>
> "A thought which does not result in an action is nothing much, and an action which does not proceed from a thought is nothing at all."
>
> —Georges Bernanos

Words are very powerful. Certainly many have been inspired, motivated and moved to action by the power of words. The intention of this book is to help the reader to clarify, choose and direct their actions. But had we not taken action, you wouldn't be reading these lines.

It's action that makes the difference. Good things may start from ideas and from the verbalization of those ideas, but action is what's needed to accomplish anything.

There are three kinds of people in this world:

1. Those who make things happen;
2. Those who watch things happen;
3. And those who wonder what happened.

Phil McGraw: "Awareness without action is worthless."

 It's OK to talk about what you believe and to talk about what you're *going* to do, but be sure you *do something*. The Universe rewards action better than words. What can you do *today* to move you toward your most important objectives?

67. Getting Things Done

Studies have shown that as few as 2 out of 100 people are able to get things done without supervision. They need someone else to watch over them or be accountable to in order to complete the job at hand.

Whether it's 2 percent or 20 percent, we can all agree that the vast majority do not take the initiative and cannot be depended upon to get the job done on their own.

The self starters who take responsibility for a task or project easily stand out in any organization. Everyone knows who they are. They solve the problems and overcome the challenges. And they stick with it until it's done. They are exceptional simply because they consistently perform.

Wayne Dyer: "It's never crowded along the extra mile."

Wayne Gretzky: "Procrastination is one of the most common and deadliest of diseases, and its toll on success and happiness is heavy."

 Be the person who can get it done. Never let there be doubt that when you take on a project, you will see it through. You will achieve the objectives and complete them on time, every time.

 101 Best Ways to Save Time and Be More Effective
www.SuccessNet.org/101savetime.htm

68. Prepare Relentlessly

So much of what we see as incompetence is not for lack of talent, knowledge or skills but rather the unwillingness to prepare. Whether it's an attorney who doesn't adequately

> "I would as soon appear before an audience half clothed as half prepared."
> —Daniel Webster

prep for an upcoming argument, a speaker who doesn't practice and study for her keynote speech or a student who didn't study before a big test, it's inadequate preparation and poor planning that are to blame.

By being well prepared, we dramatically increase our confidence. An old carpenter's axiom provides us good advice, "Measure twice, cut once."

Tom Peters: "If a window of opportunity appears, don't pull down the shade."

 All preparation and no action is not good at all. But all action and no preparation isn't good either. Do what you need to do to adequately prepare for what you do. In doing so, your confidence will be higher, the job will be done better, and the results will speak for themselves.

69. Be Flexible

Set your goals in concrete and your plans in sand. Stand firm in your values, but be willing to change tactics.

Phil McGraw: "Life is not a success-only journey. Even the best-laid plans sometimes must be altered and changed."

Jack Welch: "Change before you have to."

 Be open to input and consider viable alternatives. Be willing to make changes.

70. Hard Work

We know many people who work hard, yet don't seem to be successful. But we also know that all of the "101 Most Successful" worked hard. From this we can deduct: All success requires hard work, but not all hard work results in success. It must be the *right* work with the right purpose and the many other things outlined in this book.

> "I can't imagine a person becoming a success who doesn't give this game of life everything he's got."
> —Walter Cronkite
>
> "God sells us all things at the price of labor."
> —Leonardo da Vinci

Stephen King: "Talent is cheaper than table salt. What separates the talented individual from the successful one is a lot of hard work."

It may not be all it takes to get ahead in the world, but you're not going to get very far *without* hard work. There's no shortcut to the top. There may be better ways to do things, but there's no shortcut that circumvents hard work.

Ronald Reagan: "We cannot stop at the foothills when Everest lies ahead."

 Be unafraid of hard work. You will hardly remember it when you realize the satisfaction of your achievements. It will not seem like hard work at all.

71. Forget About "The Good Ole Days"

Too much time and energy is wasted lamenting days gone by.

The fact is, the 'Good Ole Days' were not really all that good. Things are better today than ever before. We only *think* things were better back when.

> "Don't look back on happiness, or dream of it in the future. You are only sure of today; do not let yourself be cheated out of it."
> —Henry Ward Beecher

This is the best time there is because it's the only time we have. The past is gone. Our future is not even a promise. But today—right now we *do* have.

Marianne Williamson: "God exists in eternity. The only point where eternity meets time is in the present. The present is the only time there is."

Oprah Winfrey: "Living in the moment means letting go of the past and not waiting for the future. It means living your life consciously, aware that each moment you breathe is a gift."

Wayne Dyer: "The more I give myself permission to live in the moment and enjoy it without feeling guilty or judgmental about any other time, the better I feel about the quality of my work."

 Make the best of the circumstances you find yourself in today. Waste no time wishing for some time in the past. Take hold of today and make it your best day yet. If you do, you'll look back at this day as a good one.

72. Don't Worry, Be Happy

There's no payoff to worry. If you're worried about something you can change, then invest your energy doing something about it. If you're worrying about something you *can't* change, you're engaged in a counterproductive and unhealthy activity.

> "Unless you kick the worry habit, it will haul you off into a financial desert where you will choke on the dust of your own regrets."
>
> —Jim Rohn

Worrying is a complete waste of time. Indulge yourself in worry, and you will become immobilized.

Mel Gibson: "The only way to maintain a moderate sum of happiness in this life is not to worry about the future or regret the past too much."

Wayne Dyer: "It makes no sense to worry about things you have no control over because there's nothing you can do about them, and why worry about things you do control? The activity of worrying keeps you immobilized."

 If you suffer from the worry habit, read the best book ever written about overcoming it—Dale Carnegie's *How to Stop Worrying and Start Living*.

73. Tolerations

We all have things in our life we put up with. We can improve our productivity and achieve more of our objectives by eliminating our tolerations.

As you make progress in doing so, what you'll find is your intolerance for your tolerations will increase. Things you used to accept and endure will no longer be allowed to exist. Once you label something as a toleration, your subconscious starts to see it as the enemy and begins to eliminate it.

Anthony Robbins: "Any time you sincerely want to make a change, the first thing you must do is to raise your standards. When people ask me what really changed my life eight years ago, I tell them that absolutely the most important thing was changing what I demanded of myself. I wrote down all the things I would no longer accept in my life, all the things I would no longer tolerate, and all the things that I aspired to becoming."

 Make a list of everything you can think of you consider to be a toleration. List both big ones and small ones. Rank them with the ones having the most negative impact on your life. Then, begin to formulate plans to knock them off. It's fun.

74. A Sense of Urgency

Hardly anything significant was ever accomplished with a casual attitude. Most great things have been achieved because of a great sense of urgency.

> "One of these days is none of these days."
> —H. G. Bohn

Yesterday is gone—forever. Today, and in fact, this moment, is all you have. Shrinking from the tasks at hand will make tomorrow even that much harder.

Jim Rohn: "Without a sense of urgency, desire loses its value."

 Take action now. If you only had six months to live, would you be as casual as you are now? We don't know how much time we have left in our brief existence on earth. Let's make the most of it. Make a sense of urgency a consistent part of the way you operate. Do it now.

75. Don't Let the Turkeys Get You Down

There will always be naysayers. It's easy to criticize, complain and ridicule—and most people do.

These are people with "mental BO." They're the kind of people who brighten up a room—by *leaving*. They're dream stealers. They've always been there, and they always will be. It's up to you not to listen to them.

Wayne Dyer: "A non-doer is very often a critic, that is, someone who sits back and watches doers, and then waxes philosophically about how the doers are doing. It's easy to be a critic, but being a doer requires effort, risk and change."

Tom Cruise: "When you become successful in any type of life, there are people who are not contributing to the motion."

 Decide whether you're going to listen to your dreams or listen to the stinking thinkers. Bet on your dreams.

76. Watch Less TV

Television can be a good thing. But for millions of people, it's a significant time waster. There are—in our opinion—*very* few shows really worth watching.

It's a matter of degree. If you're honest with yourself, you'll be able to tell if you're watching too much.

Steve Jobs: "You go to your TV to turn your brain off. You go to the computer when you want to turn your brain on."

 Look through the TV schedule early in the week, and carefully select those shows you want to watch or record for later viewing. Otherwise, you'll find yourself flipping channels and surfing through mindless—and sometimes even harmful—programs.

77. Take Calculated Risks

All achievement involves risk. Life itself is a risk. Jim Rohn says it's so risky, we're not going to get out alive.

> "To avoid criticism, do nothing, say nothing, be nothing."
> —Elbert Hubbard

But if you don't try, if you don't take risks, you're not going to accomplish much.

Sure people who try and fail are criticized. But that's a risk worth taking, too.

The irony is that the person not taking risks feels the same amount of fear as the person who regularly takes risks.

Marianne Williamson: "Love is what we were born with. Fear is what we learned here."

Bill Cosby: "In order to succeed, your desire for success should be greater than your fear of failure."

Sally Ride: "All adventures, especially into new territory, are scary."

Wayne Gretzky: "You miss 100% of the shots you never take."

Robert Schuller: "I would rather attempt something great and fail than attempt to do nothing and succeed."

Julia Cameron: "Leap and the net will appear."

 Become a calculated risk-taker. Not for risk's sake, but it's what's required in order to move ahead.

78. First Things First

To really get ahead in the world, you need to become good at determining what the most important things to do are and then do them. We're all busy. We all fill our lives with *something*. But is it what's most important?

> "It does not take much strength to do things, but it requires great strength to decide on what to do."
> —Elbert Hubbard

Barbara Bush: "At the end of your life, you will never regret not having passed one more test, not winning one more verdict or not closing one more deal. You will regret time not spent with a husband, a friend, a child or a parent."

Brian Tracy: "Perhaps the very best question you can memorize and repeat over and over, is 'what is the most valuable use of my time right now?'"

Ask yourself—*often*: What are my priorities? What's the most important thing to do now? What can I do that will have the biggest impact on the most important things in my life?

 "Rocks, Pebbles and Sand"
www.SuccessNet.org/articles/insp-rocks.htm

79. Leverage

Do you suffer from "The Atlas Syndrome?" Do you try to do it all yourself?

We applaud an independent spirit, but it's foolhardy to try to do everything by yourself. We live in an interdependent world and it makes sense to use the talents and skills of others in order to accelerate our progress and increase our ability to create value in the world.

In order to leverage ourselves, we need to learn how to delegate. We also need to be able to share the glory. If you attempt to do it all *your* way and by yourself, you will severely limit your success.

To excel, we must leverage all of our resources. Remember, teamwork makes the dream work.

Ronald Reagan: "Surround yourself with the best people you can find, delegate authority, and don't interfere."

 Commit to learning how to delegate well. Seek out joint ventures. Find others with similar interests but complementary talents, skills and experience. Develop a team, and watch your progress accelerate.

80. A Confused Mind Takes No Action

The military knows that when a soldier, sailor, marine or airman is confused, they're slow to take action, and the mission and the safety of the team is in jeopardy.

> "If you are clear about what you want, the world responds with clarity."
> —Loretta Staples

It's the same in life and in business. When we're unclear and confused, we tend not to take action—and sometimes we even take the wrong action.

It's easy for us—because we're so close to what we're doing—to assume that everything is clear and straightforward. It rarely is. It's imperative we keep things simple and remove every chance for confusion that we can.

Jim Rohn: "Take advantage of every opportunity to practice your communication skills so that when important occasions arise, you will have the gift, the style, the sharpness, the clarity and the emotions to affect other people."

 Whether it be with your kids, your boss, your staff or your customers, make sure they know *exactly* what you want them to do. Make your instructions and your requests perfectly clear. Don't confuse them with too many options, an unclear path or extraneous information.

81. Build On Your Strengths: Improve the Things You're Already Good at Doing

Many people spend too much time working on improving their competency in their weakest areas. It's not a very effective strategy.

What will have the better payoff—and result in more personal satisfaction—is the development of our best skills and talents. We're better off—and so are the people we serve—if we build on our strengths rather than trying to improve our weaknesses.

It's not that we shouldn't try to improve in all areas, but rather that we should devote most of our efforts to what will generate the most progress and position ourselves for creating the most value in the world.

We each have unique potential, and we'll never actualize it fully by working hard at those things that are not our inherent strengths.

 Hone and develop the things you're already good at doing. Make a list of all your attributes—your skills, knowledge, attitudes and talents. Determine what you're the best at doing. What have you the potential to master? Then, focus on those.

STEWARDSHIP

Now more than ever, we are called upon to be good stewards. The world has become smaller and is more easily impacted by what we do and what we don't do. Many of our "101 Most Successful" are active in environmental preservation and are concerned about *all* of our resources. Remember that everything affects everything else. Pay close attention to the following pieces of advice.

82. Take Care of What You Have

When most people talk about success, they usually speak in terms of acquiring things and achieving objectives. What's *not* talked about much is taking care of the things we already have.

> "If you would plant for days, plant flowers. If you would plant for years, plant trees. If you would plant for eternity, plant ideas."
> —unknown

It might not be as exciting as the actual acquiring of things, but it's critical we be accountable for all assets within our responsibility. We need plans and systems that help us to be good stewards.

It matters not what assets we have, they must be maintained. Everything we own or are responsible for must be cleaned, insured and repaired. If we own it, it's incumbent upon us to take good care of it.

How are you caring for your assets? Are they protected? Are they fully operational? Do they fit in with your goals and the vision for your future? Are they being fully leveraged and utilized?

Let's take excellent care of the things we care *about*.

 Make a list of all your assets. Here are some ideas to use in compiling your list:

- ☑ equipment, tools, intellectual property
- ☑ goodwill, reputation, contacts/network
- ☑ relationships, products, existing customers
- ☑ accounts receivable, cash, experiences, systems
- ☑ trademarks, website, domains, credit, health
- ☑ real estate, investment portfolio, time

If you have assets you're unable to adequately care for or use, sell, give them away or let go of them. In doing so, you make room for things in your life you can and will put to good use.

83. Back Up Your Data

Some of the most valuable assets we have today is in our data files. What's stored on our hard drives and on our networks may be the most difficult to replace if something bad happens to our media.

It's imperative to have a backup system—preferably automated—that duplicates in a secure fashion our all-important files.

 Set up a reliable method for backing up your files in a safe place. This can be done on the Web or using a removable medium that can be stored off-premises.

84. Bloom Where You're Planted

Wishing you were someone else or longing for better circumstances will not help you to get ahead. If your objective is to be in San Francisco, being upset about being in Chicago will not help.

> "People are always blaming their circumstances for what they are. I don't believe in circumstances. The people who get on in this world are the people who get up and look for the circumstances they want, and, if they can't find them, make them."
>
> —George Bernard Shaw

Those who succeed, learn early on that you must start from where you are. James Allen in *As a Man Thinketh* wrote, "My circumstances do not make me what I am, they reveal who I have chosen to be."

 Acknowledge where you are and the pluses and minuses of your circumstances. But then move on. Don't lament your circumstances. Begin where you are to change them.

85. Leave a Legacy

In the whole scheme of things, our time here on earth is extremely brief.

> "Every action of our lives touches on some chord that will vibrate in eternity."
>
> —Edwin Hubbel Chapin

What we leave behind from our brief existence is what we will be remembered for.

Tom Brokaw: "It's easy to make a buck. It's a lot tougher to make a difference."

Lee Iacocca: "No matter what you've done for yourself or for humanity, if you can't look back on having given love and attention to your own family, what have you really accomplished?"

Bob Dole: "When it's all over, it's not who you were; it's whether you made a difference."

Oprah Winfrey: "Unless you choose to do great things with it, it makes no difference how much you are rewarded or how much you have."

 Live your life in such a way as to make a *lasting* difference. Resolve to leave the world a better place than it was when you arrived. Plant trees that will not bloom while you live.

86. Think Long Term

It's a big life. There will be many times when things will look bleak and you will be discouraged. There will always be ups and downs. Neither of them last. Remember these words, "This too will pass."

 Ride out the cycles. Think long term. Trust the dance. Stay in the game.

SPIRITUALITY

The Dalai Lama: "When we meet real tragedy in life, we can react in two ways—either by losing hope and falling into self-destructive habits or by using the challenge to find our inner strength."

87. Follow Your Heart

In lots of different ways, many of the "101 Most Successful" advised to follow your heart. They believed in trusting your inner guidance.

It's not a question of having or not having intuition; it's a matter of becoming aware of it and trusting it. And the more you do it, the better you get at it.

> Inscription from a church in Sussex, England, 1730
>
> "A vision without a task is but a dream. A task without a vision is drudgery. A vision with a task is the hope of the world."

Donald Trump: "Experience taught me a few things. One is to listen to your gut, no matter how good something sounds on paper."

Anthony Robbins: "The quality of your life is the quality of your relationships."

 Follow your heart—not your emotions. Trust your inner guidance. When your heart speaks, take good notes.

88. A Faith to Live by, a Purpose to Live For and a Self to Live With

This didn't come from one of the "101 Most Successful." But it *did* come from someone for whom we have great respect—Charlie "Tremendous" Jones. And we thought it was some of the best advice we've heard.

How better to lead a life you can be proud of?

Jimmy Carter: ". . . my faith demands that I do whatever I can, wherever I am, whenever I can, for as long as I can with whatever I have to try to make a difference."

 Develop a faith to live by. Become clear on your purpose. Be the kind of person you would want others to emulate.

89. Pray

Quite a few of our "101 Most Successful" believe in the power of prayer. One person wrote, "Pray like it all depends upon God and work like it all depends on you." It's hard to argue with that advice.

Even if you don't believe in petitionary prayer, the consciousness developed by quiet and reverent contemplation provides a more creative, open and expecting position. Prayer isn't necessarily getting God to do our bidding as much as it is for us to be open to Universal Intelligence.

Jimmy Carter: "I have one life and one chance to make it count for something . . . I'm free to choose what that something is, and the something I've chosen is my faith. Now, my faith goes beyond theology and religion and requires considerable work and effort."

George W. Bush: "Prayer has consoled us in sorrow and will help strengthen us for the journey ahead."

 Take time to pray. Reflect upon what you want, what you can give and what you have. Ask for wisdom. Ask for solutions. Ask for belief. Ask for ideas, information and insight. Then, go to work with the expectancy you have access to all these things. Because you do.

90. Be, Do, Have—Not Do, Have, Be

Most people would think that to truly be successful, you must first do certain things, and then you will have the things you want and then you'll *be* successful.

But our "101 Most Successful" don't seem to think it works that way. Most think you must be a person who is successful and then what you do and what you attain comes into existence.

Christina Archibald wrote that if you spend more time being and less time doing, you will get more done in less time.

Stephen Covey: "We are not human beings on a spiritual journey; we are spiritual beings on a human journey."

 Be the person you truly are. In doing so, you'll live into that person with your doingness and your havingness. And you'll never be disappointed with the results.

91. Believe in Yourself

Without exception, everyone who has become successful believed in themselves enough to overcome challenges and excel in some way.

You have unique potential. No one who has come before you, and no one who will come after you was or will be exactly like you. You have special talents, skills, experiences, ideas and values. It's incumbent upon you to discover and use these unique attributes. In doing so, you'll most assuredly make a difference.

Marianne Williamson's famous quote (often erroneously attributed to Nelson Mandela): "Our deepest fear is not that we are inadequate. Our deepest fear is that we are powerful beyond measure. It is our Light, not our Darkness, that most frightens us. We ask ourselves, who am I to be brilliant, gorgeous, talented, fabulous? Actually, who are you *not* to be? You are a child of God. Your playing small does not serve the world. There is nothing enlightening about shrinking so that other people won't feel unsure around you. We were born to make manifest the glory of God that is within us. It is not just in some of us; it is in everyone. As we let our own Light shine, we unconsciously give other people permission to do the same. As we are liberated from our own fear, our presence automatically liberates others."

Barbara Bush: "If human beings are perceived as potentials rather than problems, as possessing strengths instead of weaknesses, as unlimited rather than dull and unresponsive, then they thrive and grow to their capabilities."

Mohammad Ali: "It's a lack of faith that makes people afraid of meeting challenges, and I believe in myself."

Anthony Robbins: "If you develop the absolute sense of certainty that powerful beliefs provide, then you can get yourself to accomplish virtually anything, including those things that other people are certain are impossible."

Align yourself with people who believe in you. Focus on your best qualities and don't worry about the things you're *not* so good at.

92. Gratefulness

The word appreciate has several meanings. One is to be thankful or show gratitude. Another is to raise or increase in value—such as how a good investment appreciates with time. By appreciating—practicing gratefulness—the things we have and want in our lives also increase.

> "If you learn to appreciate more of what you already have, you'll find yourself having more to appreciate."
> —Michael Angier

In our hectic, fast-paced lives, it's easy to forget about the many things for which we have to be grateful. We tend to be goal-seeking, achievement-oriented people.

And there's nothing wrong with that.

However, it's vitally important that we not lose sight of the things that are near and dear—things we all too easily take for granted.

What we focus on expands. If we focus on the problems in our lives, they tend to increase. If we focus on the good things we already have, they, too, have a tendency to grow.

We see it as another form of prayer. When we worry and fret over things, we make them bigger than they really are, as well as attract more of the same. That's negative prayer—prayer in reverse.

Oprah Winfrey: "Keep a grateful journal. Every night, list five things that happened this day that you are grateful for. What it will begin to do is change your perspective of your day and your life. If you can learn to focus on what you have, you will always see that the universe is abundant; you will have more. If you concentrate on what you don't have, you will never have enough."

Brian Tracy: "Develop an attitude of gratitude and give thanks for everything that happens to you, knowing that every step forward is a step toward achieving something bigger and better than your current situation."

 Just before going to sleep each night, think of at least three things for which you're thankful. We call it doing our "gratefuls." It takes only a few moments, but it directs our thoughts on the good—on the things we wish to increase in our life. Make the conscious consideration of your blessings a daily rather than yearly occurrence. If you do, you'll find them taking on an even greater presence.

93. Giving and Receiving

Billy Graham says, "We are not cisterns made for hoarding, we are channels made for sharing. God has given us two hands, one to receive with and the other to give with."

It's not necessarily better to give than receive. Giving and receiving is a cycle. You cannot have one without the other. If you don't receive well, you'll likely be unable to give well.

Pope John Paul II: "Anything done for another is done for oneself."

The Dalai Lama: "Our prime purpose in this life is to help others. And if you can't help them, at least don't hurt them."

Barbara Bush: "Giving frees us from the familiar territory of our own needs by opening our mind to the unexplained worlds occupied by the needs of others."

Maya Angelou: "I have found that among its other benefits, giving liberates the soul of the giver."

Brian Tracy: "Successful people are always looking for opportunities to help others. Unsuccessful people are always asking, "What's in it for me?"

 Learn to be part of the giving and receiving cycle by giving well and receiving well. Stay in the flow.

94. Respect the Earth

With over 6 billion people on the planet, we must all become good stewards. We each need to do our part to protect our home. After all, it's the only one we have.

At the very least, we should do no harm to our fragile environment. But because not everyone does this, we must also *do* something that helps preserve our water, air and land.

Kofi Annan: "We need to think of the future and the planet we are going to leave to our children and their children."

 What do you do to protect and help our earth? What are you willing to do? And what *will* you do?

GENERAL

Advice in this area either didn't fit into the above categories or was broad enough to be included in most of them. They are still worthy of our study and our attention.

95. Embrace Change

No one needs to tell you that we live in a time of unprecedented change. Those who resist change will be left behind by those who embrace it.

> **The Serenity Prayer**
>
> "God, grant me the serenity to accept the things I cannot change, the courage to change the things I can, and the wisdom to know the difference."

Change is rarely comfortable. But the more you see it as the norm and the more you accept it without judging it, the more successful you'll become. In addition, you'll be happier because it's the resistance to change that creates the pain and discomfort.

Many fortunes have been made by taking quick advantage of trends. When you see change as your friend rather than your enemy, you'll place yourself far ahead of the pack.

Muhammad Ali: "The man who views the world at 50 the same as he did at 20 has wasted 30 years of his life."

 Start looking for the good in the changes that happen around you. You may be able to change *some* things, but trying to change things you can't will result in frustration and misdirected efforts.

96. Denial is Not a Big, Long River in Egypt

You can't change what you don't acknowledge. And yet so many people live in denial. They can't or aren't willing to see the things that are usually so obvious to others. Either way, they're stuck.

That's why it's so important to get honest, educated and helpful feedback from people you trust.

Michael Crichton wrote: "The greatest challenge facing mankind is the challenge of distinguishing reality from fantasy, truth from propaganda. Perceiving the truth has always been a challenge to mankind, but in the information age (or as I think of it, the disinformation age) it takes on a special urgency and importance."

Robert Kiyosaki says, "A lot of people are afraid to tell the truth, to say no. That's where toughness comes into play. Toughness is not being a bully. It's having backbone."

 Hang around people who will tell you the truth with compassion. Be honest with yourself. Acknowledge the good, the bad and the ugly. And then make plans to do something about the things you want to change.

97. Think

Just having thoughts is not thinking. Thinking is hard work. It's asking questions. It's exploring options. It's observing and reflecting upon what you observe. It's defining problems and coming up with solutions to those problems.

> "Rarely do we find men who willingly engage in hard, solid thinking. There is an almost universal quest for easy answers and half-baked solutions. Nothing pains some people more than having to think."
>
> —Martin Luther King, Jr.

We're used to being entertained. We're used to having others think *for* us. We spend most of our life passively observing.

Thinking is often messy and uncomfortable. It's usually hard work. Perhaps that's why so few people engage in it.

Robert Allen writes, "You are the fruit of the thoughts you have planted and nourished. If you want a better harvest, you must plant better thoughts."

Edward de Bono: "Many highly intelligent people are poor thinkers, many people of average intelligence are skilled thinkers. The power of the car is separate from the way the car is driven."

 Schedule time to think. Be sure to provide opportunities to challenge your mind. What you don't use, you lose. The more you think, the better you'll get at it.

 The Lost Art of Thinking
www.SuccessNet.org/articles/angier-thinking.htm

98. Embark Upon a Lifelong Quest for Knowledge

The old cliché "Knowledge is power" isn't quite accurate. It's actually the *use* of knowledge that's power. But you can't use it unless you have it.

Most people's education ceases when they complete their formal education. It wasn't enough in the last century and it certainly isn't enough in this century. You need to constantly be educating and reeducating yourself.

> "You can't learn less."
> —Buckminster Fuller
>
> "We have two ends connected by a common middle. On one we sit and one we think. Success depends on which we use. Heads we win and tails we lose."
> —unknown

Not all readers are leaders, but all leaders are readers.

Nelson Mandela: "Education is the most powerful weapon which you can use to change the world."

Maya Angelou: "Education helps one cease being intimidated by strange situations."

 Expand your vocabulary. Read and study current events. Develop your specialized knowledge as well as your general knowledge. Take classes. Attend seminars. Always be expanding your knowledge.

99. Learn from Mistakes

Most people go through life trying to avoid mistakes. But all successful people make mistakes. And most of them have failed miserably at one thing or another. The difference is, they didn't let these setbacks stop them. They learned and moved on.

> "Your success depends upon good judgment. And how do you gain good judgment? That's easy, BAD judgment."
> —unknown
>
> "The greatest mistake we make is living in constant fear that we will make one."
> —John Maxwell

Experience is a good teacher, but it's also expensive. It's better to learn from the mistakes of others. They've been laid out for you in biographies and autobiographies and are available to us for our education.

There's no shame in making a mistake. There's only shame in making the same mistakes over again or making mistakes we have seen others make.

Robert Kiyosaki, author of "Rich Dad, Poor Dad", says "Sometimes you win and sometimes you learn."

Michael Jordan: "I've missed more than 9,000 shots in my career. I have lost almost 300 games. On 26 occasions I've been entrusted to take the game winning shot . . . and missed. And I have failed over and over and over again in my life. And that's why I succeed."

Donald Trump: "I try to learn from the past, but I plan for the future by focusing exclusively on the present. That's were the fun is."

Promise yourself that you'll not judge yourself harshly for making mistakes. Look at them as the learning experience they are. And then plan how you'll respond differently next time.

Going Broke—I Know What it's Like to Lose the Farm
www.SuccessNet.org/members/articles/angier-broke.htm

100. Balance

Over and over, our "101 Most Successful" emphasized having balance in one's life. It's something that

> "Nothing to excess."
> —Ben Franklin

almost everyone agrees with but few actually achieve.

One wise person said, "There's more to balance than not falling over."

We're not even sure it's possible *all* the time. The best one can hope for is to strike a balance in a lifetime. It's one of the reasons we categorized our sage suggestions into different areas. We were trying to promote a sense of balance.

Family and home, finances and career, mental and educational, health and fitness, community and service, spirit—these are all different areas of our lives. And yet, they make up a *whole* life. If all our goals and efforts are in only one or two areas, it's unlikely we'll feel fulfilled. When we don't round out our life, our lives don't roll along very well.

Lee Iacocca: "No matter what you've done for yourself or for humanity, if you can't look back on having given love and attention to your own family, what have you really accomplished?"

Pope John Paul II: "Man always travels along precipices. His truest obligation is to keep his balance."

Brian Tracy: "Just as your car runs more smoothly and requires less energy to go faster and farther when the wheels are in perfect alignment, you perform better when your thoughts, feelings, emotions, goals and values are in balance."

Oprah Winfrey: "Before you agree to do anything that might add even the smallest amount of stress to your life, ask yourself: What is my truest intention? Give yourself time to let a yes resound within you. When it's right, I guarantee that your entire body will feel it."

 Do your best to live a balanced life. It's never wise to have all your eggs in one basket, and it's never smart to put all your efforts into one area of your life. Live a well-rounded life.

101. Keep it Simple

Several of our "101 Most Successful" offered caution in making things too complicated.

Remember that some of the most profound concepts are the simplest. Some of the most elegant solutions are not complicated but simple. The clearest instructions are the simplest. The best speeches ever given lacked complexity. They communicated in a straightforward fashion. Short, simple sentences are more powerful than long, convoluted ones.

Lee Iacocca: "You can have brilliant ideas, but if you can't get them across, your ideas won't get you anywhere."

Warren Buffet: "The business schools reward difficult complex behavior more than simple behavior, but simple behavior is more effective."

 Break things down to their lowest common denominator. Make the complicated more understandable. Keep it simple. In doing so, you'll have better focus and position yourself to get ahead in the world.

 The Rule of Three
www.SuccessNet.org/articles/angier-ruleof3.htm

The 101 Most Successful

No one-page bio of these successful and respected people can do full justice to their lives and their accomplishments. We've strived to give you a brief sketch of who they are, some of their many accomplishments and why they made it onto this list.

In addition, we've included links to their web sites, related resources and books written by them and/or about them in order that you can dig deeper into these interesting people.

We've done our best to present the information about our "101 Most Successful" as fairly and accurately as we could. Please let us know if you find inaccuracies, so we may make corrections and improve future editions of this book.

1. Bill Gates

Born in 1955 in Seattle, Washington, USA

Occupation: chairman of Microsoft, philanthropist

Claim to Fame: the man behind "a computer in every home"

Obstacles Faced: the personal computer industry barely existed when he set out

Achievements: one of the wealthiest individuals in the history of the planet, helped bring technology to the masses, has donated billions to charities

Family: married, with 2 children

Story: This is a story of a school-age boy, the son of an attorney and a teacher, with a fascination for computers. The original computer geek, Bill Gates began programming simple games in grade school. Eventually he developed Basic, the programming language for the first microcomputer.

Gates never made it to graduation from Harvard. He focused his energy on his and Paul Allen's company—a then-small Microsoft. Gates and Allen were driven by the belief that every home and office would need a personal computer; thus, the company was born.

Microsoft's success is unparalleled. It has virtually redefined entre-preneurial success. With revenues of over $30 billion for 2003, Microsoft employs more than 55,000 people in 85 countries. A bil-lionaire at 31, and presently one of the wealthiest men in the world (his estimated worth stands at approximately $75 billion), Bill Gates is a 20th-century visionary whose unbelievable goal, "a computer in every home" became reality.

This billionaire business man is also one-half of the Bill & Melinda Gates Foundation, an organization driven by a mission to improve the standard of living for underprivileged people. Gates has greatly contributed to the Global Fund for Children's Vaccines with $750 million in grants and launched the Gates Millennium Scholars Pro-gram, awarding scholarships to low-income children. He has also donated $200 million in computers and internet access to low-income public libraries.

www.microsoft.com

Hard Drive: Bill Gates and the Making of the Microsoft Empire

The Road Ahead

2. Oprah Winfrey

Born in 1954 in Mississippi, USA

Occupation: media mogul

Claim to Fame: major media force and an inspiration to millions

Obstacles Faced: an abusive childhood in poverty, the glass ceiling faced by women and minority professionals

Achievements: named the most powerful person in show business by *Time;* recognized with numerous awards, Emmys, broadcasting awards and People's Choice awards; inducted into the Television Hall of Fame

Family: never married (happily), maintains a long-time partnership

Story: Oprah. The name instantly conjures up the woman. Her face, her personality, her accomplishments, her empathy. Leader, philanthropist, brand, media mogul and inspiration to tens of millions of people daily, Oprah is living testimony to the power of believing in your potential to overcome any obstacles.

The abused, poor, shy black girl found her way to the top. Now a strong, respected leader in several media, she has a net worth of more than $1 billion. Oprah Winfrey's fame and wealth rest on the solid foundation of connecting with others who struggle and offering them something of herself.

She is the first African American to own her own TV studio and also owns her own movie production company.

In 1991 she proposed federal child protection legislation designed to keep nationwide records on convicted abusers. In addition, Winfrey pursued a ruling that would guarantee strict sentencing of individuals convicted of child abuse. The result was a bill signed by President Clinton that allows child-care providers to check the background of prospective employees.

www.oprah.com
www.time.com/time/time100/artists/profile/winfrey.html
www.achievement.org/autodoc/page/win0bio-1
The Uncommon Wisdom of Oprah Winfrey: A Portrait in Her Own Words
Oprah Winfrey: The Soul and Spirit of a Superstar

3. Nelson Mandela

Born in 1918 in Transkei, South Africa

Occupation: freedom fighter, former president of South Africa

Claim to Fame: endured almost three decades in prison to then be freed and elected as his country's leader

Obstacles Faced: legislated racism

Achievements: considered one of the world's most respected leaders; 1993's Nobel Peace Prize; dozens of humanitarian awards, numerous honorary degrees

Story: In a life that symbolizes the triumph of the human spirit over man's inhumanity to man, Nelson Mandela accepted the 1993 Nobel Peace Prize on behalf of all South Africans who suffered and sacrificed so much to bring peace to their land.

University educated, he qualified in law in 1942. He joined the African National Congress in 1944 and committed his life to fighting against apartheid—the government-controlled regime of racial segregation.

In 1963, when many fellow leaders of the ANC were arrested, Mandela was brought to stand trial with them for plotting to overthrow the government. His statement from the dock received considerable international publicity. Eight of the accused, including Mandela, were sentenced to life imprisonment.

During his 27 years in maximum-security prison, Nelson Mandela's reputation grew steadily. He was widely accepted as the most significant black leader in South Africa and became a symbol of resistance as the anti-apartheid movement gathered strength. He consistently refused to compromise his political position to obtain his freedom.

To international celebration, Nelson Mandela was finally released on February 18, 1990. In 1991, at the first national conference of the ANC held inside South Africa after the organization had been banned in 1960, Mandela was elected president of the ANC. He was the first democratically elected president of South Africa.

www.nobel.se
www.anc.org.za/people/mandela.html
www.nobel.se/peace/laureates/1993/mandela-bio.html
Long Walk to Freedom: The Autobiography of Nelson Mandela
Mandela: An Illustrated Autobiography

4.   President George W. Bush

Born in 1946 in New Haven, Connecticut, USA

Occupation: 43rd U.S. president, won 2004 election for second presidential term

Claim to Fame: U.S. president

Obstacles Faced: America attacked by terrorists on his watch

Achievements: governor of Texas, American president

Family: married to Laura Welch Bush, with twin daughters

Story: George W. Bush was sworn into office January 20, 2001 as the 43rd President of the United States. President Bush served for six years as the 46th Governor of Texas, where he earned a reputation as a compassionate conservative who shaped public policy, based on the principles of limited government, personal responsibility, strong families and local control.

President Bush grew up in Midland and Houston, Texas. He received a bachelor's degree from Yale University in 1968, then served as an F-102 fighter pilot in the Texas Air National Guard. President Bush received an M.B.A. from Harvard Business School in 1975. After graduating, he moved back to Midland and began a career in the energy business. After working on his father's successful 1988 presidential campaign, he assembled the group of partners that purchased the Texas Rangers baseball franchise in 1989.

The tragedies of September 11, 2001 occurred just eight months into his presidency and totally altered the direction of his administration, the economic and emotional landscape of America and the foreign policy of the U.S.

Fighting terrorism, waging and managing war, strengthening home-land security and boosting the economy have become the primary directives of the Bush administration.

Being president of a super power at any time is a great challenge; during the most tumultuous and dangerous time in recent history, good leadership is vital. Although his almost every move sparks controversy and furious debate, President Bush maintains his mission: to safely bring America through these troubled times.

www.whitehouse.gov/president/gwbbio.html

A Matter of Character: Inside the White House of George W. Bush

George W. Bush: On God and Country

5. President Jimmy Carter

Born in 1924 in Georgia, USA

Occupation: 39th U.S. president, founder of the Carter Center, humanitarian, author, conflict mediator

Claim to Fame: 39th U.S. president, Nobel Peace Prize

Obstacles Faced: economic recession on his watch

Achievements: governor of Georgia, elected U.S. president, awarded the Nobel Peace Prize in 2002

Family: married to Rosalyn, with three children

Story: In 1962, Jimmy Carter entered state politics, and eight years later he was elected governor of Georgia. Among the new, young southern governors, he attracted attention by emphasizing ecology, efficiency in government and the removal of racial barriers.

Inaugurated as the 39th American president in 1977, Carter spent four years, during a time of recession and serious setback for the U.S., working to combat the continuing economic woes of inflation and unemployment, protecting the environment while dealing with a critical energy shortage.

Perhaps a greater, ongoing contribution is the non-profit Carter Center, founded in 1982 by Carter and his wife Rosalyn. The Carter Center mission is to strengthen democracy, protect and advance human rights, resolve armed political conflicts, initiate global development and health programs.

Lead by the Carters themselves, the team at the Carter Center actively works to protect and advance human rights and to alleviate human suffering. The Atlanta-based Center has helped to improve the quality of life for literally hundreds of millions of people in more than 65 countries. Their mission statement says, "The Center's staff wage peace, fight disease, and build hope by both engaging with those at the highest levels of government and working side by side with poor and often forgotten people."

www.cartercenter.org
www.whitehouse.gov/history/presidents/jc39.html
www.americanpresidents.org
An Hour Before Daylight: Memoirs of a Rural Boyhood
The Personal Beliefs of Jimmy Carter: Winner of the 2002 Nobel Peace Prize

6. Warren Buffet

Born in 1930 in Omaha, Nebraska, USA

Occupation: investor, author, philanthropist

Claim to Fame: the world's most successful investor

Achievements: his company, Berkshire Hathaway, has outperformed market benchmarks such as the S&P 500 and the DJIA for over 40 years; numerous business and financial accolades; the Buffett Foundation has won several awards for its contributions

Story: A living legend in the financial world, Warren Buffet is nicknamed the "Oracle of Omaha." He's often ranked as the second-richest person on earth, after Microsoft Chairman Bill Gates.

Buffet customarily invests in undervalued companies with low costs and good growth potential for the long term. Identifying such companies is the difficult part, but he has the knack.

His first investment was in real estate. At the age of 14, with savings from his two paper routes, he spent $1,200 on 40 acres of Nebraska farmland, which he leased to a tenant farmer.

In 1957, he started his investment partnership, putting in his own money and raising additional investments from friends and family. By 1969, he had returned an average of almost 30% a year, in a market where 7% to 11% is the norm. In his personal life, he's famously frugal. Through the Buffet Foundation, he makes charitable donations—usually around $12 million a year. He has stated his intention to disburse 99% of his wealth after his death to charity.

Susan Buffet, the billionaire investor's wife, died at the end of July 2004. She held about $2.6 billion of Berkshire Hathaway stock at the time of her death and bequeathed the bulk of this fortune to the Buffet Foundation, of which she was president. The transaction will make the Buffet Foundation the largest in the country—eclipsing the $27 million currently in the coffers of computer magnate Bill Gates' foundation.

Meanwhile, Warren Buffet, 73, has said his stock in Berkshire—worth roughly $40 billion—will also go to the Buffet Foundation upon his death.

www.buffettsecrets.com/warren-buffett-biography.htm

www.forbes.com

The Warren Buffet Way

7. Donald Trump

Born in 1946 in New York City, USA

Occupation: real estate developer, producer, author

Claim to Fame: symbol of American wealth and luxury

Obstacles Faced: bankruptcy

Achievements: developed some of the landmark buildings and projects in America, recognized for his contributions to NYC

Family: engaged to be married in early 2005 for the third time

Story: With an innate eye for business, the nature of a risk-taker and the training he received in school and while working for his father, Donald Trump knew what he wanted to do with his life. Whatever it was, he knew it would be big.

Trump transformed himself into one of the most powerful business moguls during the material heydays of the 1980s, with substantial investments in real estate, transportation, casinos and entertainment. But the financial picnic of the 80's couldn't last; stormy financial weather was on its way.

Despite his uncanny knack for making deals and recognizing a good investment when he saw one, Trump's billion-dollar empire crumbled in 1990, when he was forced into bankruptcy for over $2 billion in bank loans he couldn't pay.

Remarkably and famously, "The Donald" managed to bounce back by the end of the 1990s. He shared his story in the book, *The Art of the Comeback,* and has made a name for himself in the publishing world by co-authoring several other popular books about himself.

Thanks to the popular hit NBC reality series, *The Apprentice,* in which 16 contestants vie for a position at one of Trump's corporations, The Donald can add television success to his achievements.

Trump rose up, fell down and got back up in a big way. Whether empire-building, going bankrupt or making a notorious comeback, Trump's style, inspiration, passion and modus operendi was, is and ever shall be: to Think Big.

www.askmen.com
Trump: How to Get Rich
Trump: The Art of the Deal
Trump: The Way to the Top—The Best Business Advice I Ever Received

8. Anthony Robbins

Born in 1960 in Los Angeles, California, USA

Occupation: speaker, trainer, coach, author

Claim to Fame: the most widely recognized expert on personal development

Obstacles Faced: poverty, health issues

Achievements: has directly impacted the lives of nearly 50 million people from 80 countries with his best-selling books and audiotape products, public speaking engagements and live appearances

Family: married, with four children

Story: Tony Robbins is a big man. His smile is big and his charisma is bigger. His energy is big and his drive to help others is bigger. His financial success is big. His self-development empire is big. His mission to empower people to succeed is big.

His non-profit Anthony Robbins Foundation assists the homeless, elderly and inner-city youth and feeds more than one million people in nine countries every year through its international holiday "Basket Brigade." His foundation has provided support or initiated programs in 2,046 schools, 758 prisons and more than 100,000 health and human service organizations and homeless shelters.

Robbins' companies together generate nearly half a billion dollars in revenue per year.

International leaders, including President Clinton, Nelson Mandela, Mikhail Gorbachev, Margaret Thatcher, Francois Mitterand, Princess Diana and Mother Theresa have sought his strategic advice and counsel. He has consulted members of two royal families, U.S. congressmen, the U.S. Army, the U.S. Marines and three presidents of the United States.

www.anthonyrobbins.com
Awaken the Giant Within
Unlimited Power: The New Science Of Personal Achievement

9. Dr. Stephen Covey

Born in 1932 in Salt Lake City, Utah, USA

Occupation: author, speaker, teacher, consultant, mentor

Claim to Fame: in 2002, *Forbes* named his book, *The 7 Habits of Highly Effective People,* one of the top ten most influential management books ever

Achievements: a variety of accolades for his contribution to management and leadership theories

Family: married, with nine children

Story: Dr. Stephen R. Covey's life is a portrait of achievement in the never-ending improvement of business, government and education. To experience Covey, either by reading his books, attending a seminar or taking a course, is to become a follower.

For over a quarter of a century, Dr. Covey has taught hundreds of organizations how to better manage and how to effectively lead. His work in principle-centered leadership has altered the business and governmental landscape with his inside-out approach to improving the quality of service, leadership, innovation and teamwork.

He's founder and chairman of the Covey Leadership Center, an international organization whose mission is to empower people and organizations to significantly increase their performance capability in order to achieve worthwhile purposes through understanding and living principle-centered leadership. Covey is also founder of The Institute for Principle Centered Leadership, a non-profit research group dedicated to transforming education and improving the quality of community life.

Dr. Covey's book, *The Seven Habits of Highly Effective People*, was a *New York Times* #1 best seller with more than 1.5 million copies sold. The book is published in over 20 countries and in a dozen languages. A survey by *Chief Executive Magazine* recognized *The 7 Habits of Highly Effective People* as one of the two most influential business books of the twentieth century. His leadership advisory magazine *Executive Excellence* is in its eighth year of publication.

www.wisdomstore.com

www.franklincovey.com

The Seven Habits of Highly Effective People

10. Pope John Paul II

Born in 1920 in Cracow, Poland

Occupation: Pope of the Roman Catholic Church

Claim to Fame: known as "the people's Pope"

Obstacles Faced: persecution of Catholics by the Nazi regime; the ever-declining numbers of Catholics worldwide

Story: Karol Józef Wojtyła has been known as John Paul II since his October 1978 election to the papacy

In 1942, aware of his call to the priesthood, he began courses in the seminary of Cracow, which was forced underground to avoid persecution by the Nazi regime. He persevered and was ordained as a priest on November 1, 1946.

Appointed Auxiliary Bishop of Cracow by Pope Pius XII in 1958 and nominated Archbishop of Cracow by Pope Paul VI in 1964, he became a cardinal in 1967.

Since the start of his Pontificate in 1978, Pope John Paul II has distinguished himself by connecting with the people like no other Pope in history. Navigating the Vatican into the modern world, he will be remembered for his popularity as well as for his achievements.

As Pope, he's conducted hundreds of pastoral visits, presided at innumerable ceremonies, authored dozens of significant apostolic writings and written three books, including a book of poems in March 2003.

No other Pope is renowned for his encounters with so many individuals. More than 17,119,200 pilgrims have participated in the general audiences with John Paul II. This figure doesn't include all the other special audiences and religious ceremonies held (more than 8 million pilgrims came to see him during the Great Jubilee of the Year 2000 alone) and the millions of faithful who met during pastoral visits made in Italy and throughout the world.

Challenged to continue his mission both by old age and by advanced Parkinson's disease, His Holiness John Paul II is adamant that he will connect with worshippers until it's no longer possible.

www.Vatican.va

Rise, Let Us Be On Our Way

Pope John Paul II: In My Own Words

11. President Bill Clinton

Born in 1946 in Hope, Arkansas, USA

Occupation: former U.S. president

Claim to Fame: popular president, impeached, acquitted

Achievements: governor of Arkansas, former president of the United States

Family: married to Senator Hillary Clinton, with one daughter

Story: William Jefferson Blythe, IV was named for his father, who died in a traffic accident three months before the birth of his son. When his mother remarried, he took the surname Clinton.

Clinton spent his youth balancing his dual passion for education (he completed law school at Yale in 1973) and politics. In 1976, Clinton was elected attorney general of Arkansas. Then, at the age of 32, he became the governor of Arkansas, the youngest governor in America. In 1993, at age 46, Clinton became the youngest man to be elected president of the United States since John F. Kennedy. Bill Clinton was the 42nd president for two consecutive terms (1993-2001).

Clinton led during a period of peace and prosperity in America. The economy was good and his policies were generally popular. Although Ronald Reagan was largely credited for the strong economy, on Clinton's watch, the country experienced 110 consecutive months of economic expansion—the longest economic expansion in history.

However, due to lying before a federal grand jury and a protracted sex-scandal that shook both his marriage and his reputation, Clinton became the second president in American history to be impeached. After a Senate trial in January and February 1999, Clinton was acquitted.

In September 2004, Clinton successfully underwent quadruple heart bypass surgery.

www.whitehouse.gov/history/presidents/bc42.html

www.americanpresidents.org/presidents/president.asp?PresidentNumber=41

My Life

First in His Class: A Biography of Bill Clinton

12. Senator Hillary Rodham Clinton

Born in 1947 in Chicago, Illinois, USA

Occupation: U.S. senator

Claim to Fame: former first lady, the first ever to become a senator

Obstacles Faced: husband's infidelity and impeachment

Family: married to Bill Clinton, with one daughter

Story: Hillary Rodham Clinton served as first lady to Arkansas for twelve years and then as America's first lady for eight.

She chaired educational and health boards and served the Children's Defense Fund. A major advocate for children, she co-founded several programs for the legal, educational and health advancement of children and families. In 1993, the President asked her to chair the Task Force on National Health Care Reform.

Mrs. Clinton recently received the Living Legacy Award from the Women's International Center for her work for women and children. In recognition of her professional and personal accomplishments, Hillary was named Arkansas Woman of the Year in 1983 and Arkansas Mother of the Year in 1984. She was named one of the nation's top 100 lawyers by the *National Law Review* in 1988 and 1991.

Hillary Clinton was elected United States senator from New York in 2000. She is the first woman elected statewide in New York and the only first lady ever elected to the U.S. senate.

www.clinton.senate.gov/about_hrc.html

www.whitehouse.gov/history/firstladies/hc42.html

Living History

It Takes a Village

13. Dr. Wayne Dyer

Born in 1940 in Detroit, Michigan, USA

Occupation: popular lecturer, psychotherapist, best-selling author

Claim to Fame: one of the most widely known and respected people in the field of self empowerment

Achievements: overcame adversity to create a good life and teaches others to do the same, elected to the International Speakers Hall of Fame and awarded the prestigious Golden Gavel Award from Toast-masters International

Obstacles Faced: spent childhood in orphanages and foster homes

Family: lives with his family in southern Florida

Story: Abandoned by his parents, Dr. Dyer's childhood was endured in foster homes and orphanages. Immediately after high school, he enlisted in the U.S. Navy for four years' service. Despite the difficult upbringing and youth, he's worked hard and visioned clearly to create the life of his dreams. A doctor of counseling psychotherapy, he's the author of *Your Erroneous Zones, Pulling Your Own Strings, You'll See It When You Believe It* and *Real Magic.*

Dr. Dyer has been published in numerous national publications, and he's the author of many best-selling audiocassette programs. He has appeared on over 5,200 television and radio programs.

Wayne Dyer describes his early life as absolutely perfect, because it led him to where he is today.

www.drwaynedyer.com/home

The Power of Intention: Learning to Co-Create Your World Your Way

10 Secrets for Success and Inner Peace

Your Erroneous Zones

Real Magic

14. The Dalai Lama

Born in 1935 in China

Occupation: the spiritual leader of Tibet

Claim to Fame: the reincarnation of each of the previous thirteen Dalai Lamas of Tibet, the first having been born in 1351 AD

Obstacles Faced: at 15, he was leader of six million people facing the threat of a full-scale war with communist China, invasion and occupation of his country by China; the systematic murder of hundreds of thousands of Tibetans; living in exile for half a century

Achievements: building a reputation as a respected world-leader and spiritual teacher while living in exile from his country; numerous humanitarian awards, honorary degrees, lifetime achievement awards, peace awards, Nobel Peace Prize, honorary citizenship of Texas, dozens of international awards and environmental awards

Story: When poor Tibetan villager Lhamo Thondup was barely three years old, a search party was sent out by the Tibetan government to find the new incarnation of the Dalai Lama came to his village. The boy recognized the leader of the search party, as well as several objects belonging to the previous Dalai Lama. Following ancient tradition, the boy was officially recognized as the reincarnation of the Dalai Lama and trained to become the leader of the country.

At a young age, he stepped into a position of power and into a very violent and troubled age for Tibet. After years of unsuccessful peace talks and a violent suppression of Tibet's resistance movement in which tens of thousands of Tibetans died, Tibet was occupied by communist China in 1959. Reluctantly, and at the urging of his officials, the Dalai Lama fled to Dharamsala, India, where he continues to be the spiritual leader of Tibet's people and heads Tibet's government-in-exile. He has been in exile for 45 years.

His Holiness the Dalai Lama has always advocated peaceful solutions, based upon tolerance and mutual respect in his struggles to free Tibet and save his citizens from the repressive rule of one of the world's most powerful militaries.

www.tibet.com
www.dalailama.com/html/contents.html
www.tibet.com/DL
The Art of Happiness: A Handbook for Living
Ethics for the New Millennium: His Holiness the Dalai Lama

15. Jim Rohn

Born in 1932 in Idaho, USA

Occupation: business philosopher, motivational counselor, business executive, author

Claim to Fame: hailed as one of the most influential thinkers of our time

Achievements: recognized as one of the greatest motivational speakers of all time, awarded the CPAE Award from the National Speakers Association in 1985

Story: Jim Rohn is one of the world's most renowned success counselors and business philosophers. He leads the pack in education of subjects such as sales, business skills, leadership, success and personal development.

Over almost half a century, Rohn has addressed over four million people worldwide. He's authored over 17 different books, audio and video programs and been internationally hailed as one of the most influential thinkers of our time.

Disseminating information and inspiration on success in his unique manner that is both accessible and practical, Jim ignites enthusiasm and a belief in potential. His style of speaking and of teaching is witty and anecdotal, and it simply works to cut through the obstacles. Rohn has dedicated his life to helping others achieve their potential in life and in business.

www.SuccessNet.org/go/rohn.htm

7 Strategies for Wealth & Happiness:
Power Ideas from America's Foremost Business Philosopher

The Art of Exceptional Living

16. Dr. Billy Graham

Born in 1918 in North Carolina, USA

Occupation: Christian evangelist

Claim to Fame: most enduring and popular American preacher in history

Obstacles Faced: wavering reputation of the Christian Right, due to scandals and frauds perpetrated by other evangelists

Achievements: author of 25 top-selling books; known as the "the Pope of Protestant America"; awarded the Congressional Gold Medal (1996); the Templeton Foundation Prize for Progress in Religion (1982); the Ronald Reagan Presidential Foundation Freedom Award (2000) for contributions to the cause of freedom; in December 2001 presented with an honorary knighthood, Honorary Knight Commander of the Order of the British Empire (KBE), for his international contribution to civic and religious life over 60 years

Family: married to Ruth, with five children

Story: In America, 96% percent of the population believes in God, 90% pray, and 90% percent believe that God loves them, according to Gallup polls. According to the same polls, 40% of Americans believe God speaks to them directly. In a country where state is legislatively separate from the church, yet faith is obviously mainstream, there is a spiritual leader for millions—Billy Graham.

Graham has preached the Gospel to more people in live audiences than anyone else in history—over 210 million people in more than 185 countries.

Ubiquitously featured on the covers of *Time, Newsweek, Life* and other magazines, Graham has also written 24 books—many of them top sellers.

Founder of the Billy Graham Evangelistic Association, he stepped down in 2000 in order to continue his crusade ministry. His son, Franklin Graham, stepped into his shoes.

www.billygraham.org

Just As I Am: The Autobiography of Billy Graham

Angels

17. Dr. Deepak Chopra

Born in 1947 in New Delhi, India

Occupation: doctor, teacher, author, speaker

Claim to Fame: introduced the concepts of Ayurvedic medicine, holistic healing and the fusion of Eastern and Western healing to the mainstream

Achievements: in 1999, *Time* magazine named Chopra one of the top 100 icons and heroes of the 20th century

Family: married, with two children

Story: Deepak Chopra, M.D. is at the forefront of holistic healing. He has significantly influenced traditional medicine while helping to introduce the benefits of holistic medicine to the world. Chopra studied medicine before moving to the U.S. in 1970. He established his own practice in Boston, later teaching at Boston University and Tufts medical schools and becoming chief of staff at New England Memorial Hospital.

Renowned for his work in exploring health and healing through the integration of mind and body, he merges the best of modern science and ancient wisdom. Chopra is one of the world's leading champions of an innovative combination of eastern and western healing.

Published in 1993, his book *Ageless Body, Timeless Mind* was an instant success and sold over a million copies in hardcover alone. Possibly his most popular book, *The Seven Spiritual Laws of Success,* was published in 1994.

Spanning almost three decades of important contributions to the growing field of holistic health, self-improvement and spirituality, Deepak has written 25 books and produced more than 100 audio, video and CD-ROM projects. His books have sold 10 million copies in English alone.

www.chopra.com

www.mypotential.ie/spirit/deepak_intro.html

The Seven Spiritual Laws of Success: A Practical Guide to the Fulfillment of Your Dreams

How to Know God

The Path to Love: Spiritual Strategies for Healing

18. Zig Ziglar

Born in 1926 in Alabama, USA

Occupation: motivational speaker, author, salesman

Claim to Fame: one of the world's most popular motivational speakers

Obstacles Faced: child of The Great Depression; father passed away, leaving the young family with financial struggles

Achievements: recognized three times in the Congressional Record of the United States

Family: married to Jean

Story: After serving his country in the Navy and then attending the University of South Carolina, Hilary Hinton Ziglar began his professional life selling cookware door to door for the Wearever Aluminum Company. After a few lackluster years, he was inspired by a company executive to strive for excellence and soon set company records for sales. Tapping into his innate charm, enthusiasm and zest for life, Ziglar uncovered his true calling: motivating people to achieve their potential.

For the past 34 years, "Zig" Ziglar, a born-again Christian, has delivered his messages of self-improvement, balance, harmony and faith around the world, covering a distance of 5 million miles. His audiences have included, over the years, notable figures such as President Ford, President Reagan, President Bush, General Norman Schwarzkopf, Secretary of State Colin Powell, Dr. Norman Vincent Peale, Paul Harvey, Dr. Robert Schuller and various members of U.S. Congress and governors.

Author of 23 books, Ziglar has become an authority on leadership, faith, family and success. Nine of his books have been best sellers, and they've been translated into 38 languages. Ziglar's company, Ziglar Training Systems, offers educational programs, seminars, speakers and workshops designed for personal and professional development.

www.ziglartraining.com

www.olemiss.edu/mwp/dir/ziglar_zig

Goals : Setting and Achieving Them on Schedule

How to be a Winner

19. Sir Richard Branson

Born in 1950 in Surrey, England

Occupation: business man, philanthropist, adventurer

Claim to Fame: founder of Virgin Music, Virgin Airlines, Virgin Trains, Virgin Radio, Virgin Cola, Virgin Hotels, Virgin Books, etc.

Obstacles Faced: small thinking

Achievements: named one of the "100 Greatest Britons," Branson was knighted by the Queen for his business prowess and exuberance for the United Kingdom

Family: married, with two children

Story: Richard Branson started his entrepreneurship at a young age. He created a magazine entitled *Student* at the age of sixteen. This wasn't a high school rag or even a local publication; it was a national magazine.

At twenty years old, he founded *Virgin* as a mail order record retailer. Branson opened the first Virgin record shop in Oxford Street, London and soon added a recording studio.

In 1992, Sir Richard sold his music empire—The Virgin Music Group—to EMI in a $1 billion U.S. deal. "I remember walking down the street after I sold Virgin Records," he says. "I was crying. Tears of grief streaming down my face. And there I was, holding a check for a billion dollars." He pauses for a second, and then adds, "If you'd seen me, you would have thought I was loony. A billion dollars."

Not one to play small, Branson took a major risk in the 1980's and launched Virgin Atlantic Airways, which is now the second largest British long-haul airline and operates a fleet of Boeing 747 aircrafts to major world cities.

The combined sales of Virgin Group Companies exceed $3 billion U.S. In September 2004, Branson purchased the rights to commercial space travel. Plans to sell tickets to space to the general public by 2007 are in the works.

www.virgin.com

Sir Richard Branson: The Autobiography

*Losing My Virginity: How I've Survived,
Had Fun, and Made a Fortune Doing Business My Way*

20. General Colin Powell

Born in 1937 in New York City, USA

Occupation: U.S. secretary of state

Claim to Fame: the highest-ranking black government official in the history of the United States

Achievements: a decorated four-star general in the U.S. Army; the first African American secretary of state; recipient of 26 U.S. and foreign military awards and decorations, including the Purple Heart; in 1993, was made an honorary Knight Commander of the Order of the Bath by Queen Elizabeth II; civilian awards include two Presidential Medals of Freedom, the President's Citizens Medal, the Congressional Gold Medal, the Secretary of State Distinguished Service Medal and the Secretary of Energy Distinguished Service Medal; several schools and other institutions have been named in his honor; holds honorary degrees from universities and colleges across the country

Family: married to the former Alma Vivian Johnson of Birmingham, Alabama, with one son Michael and two daughters

Story: Colin Powell became the 65th secretary of state at the beginning of 2001, a momentous year for America. Foreshadowing the importance of U.S. foreign policy on his watch, Powell stated at his confirmation hearing that the guiding principle during his tenure will be that "America stands ready to help any country that wishes to join the democratic world."

Before stepping into office at the White House, Secretary Powell served as aid to the secretary of defense and as national security advisor. He also served 35 years in the United States Army, rising to the rank of four-star general and serving as chairman of the Joint Chiefs of Staff.

www.state.gov/secretary

www.whitehouse.gov/government/powell-bio.html

www.en.wikipedia.org/wiki/Colin_Powell

The Leadership Secrets of Colin Powell

My American Journey

21. Maya Angelou

Born Marguerite Johnson in 1928 in St. Louis, Missouri, USA

Occupation: author, poet, historian, songwriter, playwright, dancer, stage and screen producer, director, performer, singer, civil rights activist

Claim to Fame: best known for her series of autobiographical books, culminating in *I Know Why the Caged Bird Sings* (1969), which was nominated for the National Book Award

Obstacles Faced: prevalent racism, poverty

Achievements: achieved numerous 'firsts' as an African American woman. Her poetry has been nominated for the Pulitzer Prize; holds several honorary degrees and has won a variety of artistic and cultural awards

Story: An American woman of letters, who is an icon of achieving one's potential by transcending obstacles, Maya Angelou has earned her place in our cultural heritage.

In 1959, at the request of Dr. Martin Luther King, Jr., Angelou became the northern coordinator for the Southern Christian Leadership Conference. In 1974, she was appointed by Gerald Ford to the Bicentennial Commission and later by Jimmy Carter to the Commission for International Woman of the Year. In 1993, Angelou wrote and delivered a poem, "On the Pulse of the Morning," at the inauguration for President Bill Clinton at his request.

The first black woman director in Hollywood, Angelou has written, produced, directed and starred in productions for stage, film and television. Although her many accolades, awards for her writing, activism, producing and acting reflect an individual with true talent and drive, Maya Angelou is an inspiration more for who she is than for what she has accomplished.

As a woman, as an African American and as a child of poverty, she's someone whose bright spirit burns the so-called obstacles in her path. It takes an incredible effort for a black woman from poverty to succeed at every project she takes on. Angelou shows us that our only limitations are the ones we believe in.

www.poets.com
www.worldofquotes.com
The Collected Autobiographies of Maya Angelou
The Heart of a Woman

22. Margaret Thatcher

Born in 1925 in Lincolnshire, England

Occupation: former prime minister of England (1979-1990)

Achievements: first woman to become leader of the British Conservative Party; first woman prime minister of the United Kingdom, the longest-serving prime minister of the UK in the 20th century, named #16 in the 2002 List of "100 Greatest Britons" (sponsored by the BBC and voted for by the public), named #3 in the 2003 List of "100 Worst Britons" (sponsored by Channel Four and also voted for by the public)

Family: widowed in 2003, with twins

Story: In the early 1940s, Margaret Thatcher was a regular student at Oxford University, where she studied chemistry and law. At the age of 34, after having started her family, she was elected as Member of Parliament, a seat she held until her retirement from the House of Commons 23 years later. She became the England's first female prime minister on May 4, 1979.

During her time as prime minister, Margaret Thatcher became one of the most respected—and controversial—world leaders of her era. She directed her country with a famously firm hand, eliminating costly and bureaucratic-heavy social systems, encouraged open markets and brought down the notorious trade unions that were strangling businesses at the time. She moved Britain toward privatization at a time when privatization was a new term in world government. Due in part to her leadership, by the end of the 1980's more than 50 countries, on almost every continent, had set in motion privatization programs.

Thatcher won three general elections before she was voted out of office in 1990. Two years later, she and her husband were elevated to the Peerage, and she took her seat in the House of Lords as Baroness Thatcher of Kesteven. She remained active in political life and continued to lecture on behalf of the Thatcher Foundation until 2002, when doctors advised her to wind down her activities for the sake of her health.

www.margaretthatcher.com

www.number-10.gov.uk/output/page126.asp

www.time.com/time/time100/leaders/profile/thatcher.html

Margaret Thatcher: The Path to Power

The World According to Margaret Thatcher

23. Jack Welch

Born in 1935 in Salem, Massachusetts, USA

Occupation: consultant, speaker

Claim to Fame: chairman and CEO of General Electric (1981-2001)

Obstacles Faced: economic downturn, old-school business practices

Achievements: considered the most admired CEO of the most admired corporation in America

Family: married twice, with four children

Story: Jack Welch is one of the most successful business leaders of all time. He made GE the most valuable company in the history of the world. His efforts increased the market value of the company to a degree unmatched by any other CEO.

In 1960, Welch started in GE's plastics division for an annual salary of $10,500. In 1968, at the age of 33, he became GE's youngest general manager. Ten years later, he was vice chairman and executive officer of the company. Along the way, he built plastics into a formidable $2 billion business. In December 1980, Welch was announced as the new CEO and chairman of GE. It was a record-breaking appointment. At 45, Welch was the youngest chief the company had ever appointed.

Since 1981, GE sales have risen from $27.2 billion to $173.2 billion. Over the same period, profits rose from $1.6 billion to $10.7 billion. But it was perhaps the corporate culture on which Welch's legacy had the biggest influence. Welch built a business culture like no other—by cutting through the red tape and bureaucracy and developing an informal learning environment. This informal approach encourages managers to get to know the employees, interact with them and get involved in all aspects of the business.

While he's known as personable and persistent, he's also renowned for being a demanding leader—earning him the nickname "Neutron Jack." Welch stepped down as head of GE on September 7, 2001. Today he serves as a consultant to a small group of Fortune 500 business CEOs.

www.askmen.com/men/business_politics/45_jack_welch.html

www.ge.com/en/company/companyinfo/at_a_glance/bio_welch.htm

Jack: Straight from the Gut

Winning: The Ultimate Business How-To Book

24. Kofi A. Annan

Born in 1938 in Ghana, Africa

Occupation: secretary-general of the United Nations

Claim to Fame: first secretary-general to be elected from the ranks of UN staff

Achievements: Nobel Peace Prize Laureate, 2001

Family: married to Nane Lagergren, a Swedish artist and lawyer, who has authored a book for children about the United Nations, with three children

Story: Described as confident and candid, with a keen sense of humor, Kofi Annan has been a popular and familiar figure, both inside and outside the United Nations. Annan first gained international recognition during the Persian Gulf War, when he negotiated the release of UN staff in Iraq.

Educated in West Africa, Geneva and the United States, Mr. Annan joined the UN in 1962. He has received honorary degrees from universities in Africa, Asia, Europe and North America, as well as a number of other prizes and awards for his contributions to the aims and purposes of the United Nations.

Since becoming secretary-general in January 1997, Mr. Annan has given priority to restoring public confidence in the UN by, in his words, "bringing the United Nations closer to the people." He has also taken a leading role in mobilizing the international community in the battle against HIV/AIDS, and more recently, against the global terrorist threat.

Calling the HIV/AIDS epidemic his "personal priority," the secretary-general issued a "Call to Action" in April 2001, proposing the establishment of a Global AIDS and Health Fund, which has since received some $1.5 billion in pledges and contributions.

Since the terrorist attacks hit the United States on September 11, 2001, the secretary-general has played a leading role in galvanizing global action through the General Assembly and the Security Council to combat terrorism.

www.abcnews.go.com/reference/bios/annan.html
www.nobel.se/peace/laureates/2001/annan-bio.html
We the Peoples: Nobel Peace Message
United Nations and Changing World Politics

25. Dr. Phil McGraw

Born in 1950 in Oklahoma, USA

Occupation: author, speaker, television host, psychologist

Claim to Fame: bringing behavioral and psychological awareness to the mainstream

Obstacles Faced: growing up in an unstable family, with an alcoholic father

Achievements: *The Dr. Phil Show* has been making headlines and breaking records since its September 2002 launch, when it garnered the highest ratings of any new syndicated show since the launch of *The Oprah Winfrey Show*; named one of the "Most Intriguing People of 2002" by *People* magazine; Barbara Walters listed him in her 2002 "Ten Most Fascinating People" special

Family: married to Robin, his wife of 28 years, with two sons

Story: Dr. Phil earned his bachelors, masters and doctorate degrees in clinical psychology from North Texas State University and set up a private practice.

Eventually seeing that his passions lay in a different direction, he created a successful self-motivation seminar called Pathways. However, the still-questing McGraw went on to become the president and co-founder of Courtroom Sciences, Inc., a trial preparation firm.

It was as president of CSI that McGraw stepped onto the mainstream celebrity stage when he was selected by Oprah Winfrey to consult and coach her to victory in her trial against the Texas cattle ranchers, who sued her for defamation after her show on Mad Cow disease. With McGraw's help, Oprah prevailed and her reputation and career were saved, along with about $12 million in damages for which she was being sued.

Oprah gave McGraw a platform as a regular guest on her show to bring his unique brand of therapy to the public. Nicknamed Dr. Phil, his popularity skyrocketed.

McGraw is a very sought-after public speaker. He's published numerous scholarly articles in the field of clinical psychology and behavioral medicine.

www.drphil.com
Life Strategies: Doing What Works, Doing What Matters
Self Matters: Creating Your Life from the Inside Out

26. Steven Spielberg

Born in 1946 in Cincinnati, Ohio, USA

Occupation: film director

Claim to Fame: brought us such movie classics as *Jaws, Raiders of the Lost Ark* and the other *Indiana Jones* sequels, *Close Encounters of the Third Kind, E.T. The Extraterrestrial, Jurassic Park* and *Schindler's List*

Achievements: the most financially successful motion picture director of all time; in 2004 listed in *Premiere* and other magazines as the most powerful and influential figure in the motion picture industry; named Best Director of the 20th Century in an *Entertainment Weekly* online poll; awarded the Distinguished Public Service Award by the U.S. Navy for his work on *Saving Private Ryan* and the second annual John Huston Award for Artists Rights

Family: divorced from Amy Irving, with one son; married to Kate Capshaw, with six children

Story: At age 12, Steven Spielberg financed his first amateur film with the money he earned from his tree-planting business. Now his films are part of our cultural heritage.

1975's *Jaws* won four Academy Awards and earned over $100 million at the box office—a record at the time. Since then, he's been the man behind enormous box-office hits and is known as someone who has the influence, financial resources and acceptance of Hollywood studio authorities to make any film he chooses. As of 2004, he's won two Academy Awards for Best Director, one for *Schindler's List* and another for *Saving Private Ryan.*

He's not only recognized as one of the greatest filmmakers of all-time, but is also known for his charitable work for World War II organizations and the Righteous Persons Foundation. He has donated funds to various Jewish projects, especially Holocaust memorial organizations.

www.spielbergfilms.com

www.en.wikipedia.org/wiki/Steven_Spielberg

www.time.com/time/time100/artists/profile/spielberg.html

Steven Spielberg: Crazy for Movies

Steven Spielberg (A&E Biography)

27. Tiger Woods

Born in 1975 in Cypress, California, USA

Occupation: golf champion

Claim to Fame: in 1997, in his 42nd week as a professional, he became the youngest-ever #1 golfer on the Official World Golf Ranking at 21 years of age; he claims the most rapid progression ever to that position

Key Achievements: fastest player to win a million dollars on the PGA Tour (on his 9th event), fastest player to win two million dollars on the PGA Tour (on his 16th event), fastest player to win 10 million dollars on the PGA Tour (on his 69th event), *Golf Digest* Player of the Year in 1991 and 1992, Golf World Player of the Year in 1992 and 1993, Golf World Man of the Year in 1994, ESPY Male Athlete of the Year in 1997, 1999 and 2000; PGA Tour Player of the Year in 1997 and 1999; World Sportsman of the Year in 1999, 2000 by the World Sports Academy

Family: married in October 2004

Story: Eldrick Woods began playing golf at six months old. He shot 48 for nine holes at age 3 and was featured in *Golf Digest* at age five. At the age of eight, he won the first of six Optimist International Junior World Titles. Obviously, it was the beginnings of a legend. Nicknamed "Tiger" after a Vietnamese soldier who was a friend of his father's in Vietnam, the boy would go on to become the #1 ranked player in the world, outclassing the competition by a record margin.

His record of achievement reads like a long list of awards. Suffice it to say, he's earned champion status as the youngest, the fastest, the first, the highest paid, the only and the best at golf. For a young, non-Caucasian man to literally steal the game away from the status quo players—middle aged, privileged white men—simply added to his legend.

Woods has won virtually every championship in the game, often several times over and by margins that astonished the world. He is a popular and beloved athlete.

www.pga.com/pgachampionship/scoring/profiles/8793.html
www.tigerwoods.com/aboutme/bio.sps?sid=825&lid=1&aid=0
Tiger Woods: A Biography
How I Play Golf

28. Dr. John C. Maxwell

Born in 1947 in Ohio, USA

Occupation: entrepreneur, author, speaker

Claim to Fame: known as America's expert on leadership

Achievements: reaching almost 500,000 people annually via his speaking engagements, in addition to at least one million through his resources and publications; many of his titles have landed on the best-seller list in noted publications such as *The New York Times, Business Week, Wall Street Journal, USA Today* and *CBA Market-place*

Family: lives in Atlanta, Georgia with his wife Margaret

Story: John Maxwell's faith, combined with his charisma and a driving passion to reach out to people, led him to follow his spiritual calling. First as a pastor, and later as an authority on Christian leadership, Maxwell built his solid reputation on his search for a winning pairing of leadership skills and personal spirituality.

In 1985, after 16 years as a pastor, Maxwell founded INJOY®, an organization that provides Christian leaders with programs and resources for personal development, stewardship and leadership. In 1995, he resigned his pastorate in order to devote his time and energy to the company he founded.

Along with hosting and teaching at INJOY® conferences, John speaks frequently for several high-profile organizations such as Promise Keepers, Focus on the Family, Sam's Club and various Fortune 500 companies.

www.maximumimpact.com

www.injoy.com

Developing the Leader Within You

The 21 Irrefutable Laws of Leadership

29. Mark Victor Hansen

Born in Waukegan, Illinois, USA

Occupation: author, speaker

Claim to Fame: co-authored the *Chicken Soup for the Soul* book series

Achievements: given over 5,000 presentations to more than 2 million people in 32 countries, honored with the prestigious Horatio Alger Award, received the Outstanding Business Leader of the Year award from Northwood University, awarded an honorary Ph.D. in Business Administration from the University of Toledo

Family: married to Patty

Story: Mark Victor Hansen is a professional speaker who, in the last 30 years, has inspired literally hundreds of thousands of people to create a more powerful and purposeful future for themselves. And while he was at it, stimulating the sale of billions of dollars worth of goods and services.

Most famous for creating the popular *Chicken Soup for the Soul* books, the series now boasts more than 90 titles and a variety of related products. The billion-dollar enterprise was named by *Time* magazine "the publishing phenomenon of the decade." With sales well over 85 million copies, it has become the most successful non-fiction book series in America.

Hansen's next work, to be published in 2005, is the sequel to the popular *One Minute Millionaire,* entitled *The Last Minute Millionaire.* It's already marked as a sure-fire best seller.

Mark is a founding member of the National Speakers Association and has appeared on *Oprah*, CNN, *Eye to Eye* and the *Today Show.* He has also been featured in *Time, US News and World Report, USA Today, The New York Times, Entrepreneur, Success, Forbes, Working Woman* and *People* magazines.

www.markvictorhansen.com

www.premierespeakers.com/823/index.cfm

Multiple Streams of Income: How to Generate a Lifetime of Unlimited Wealth

The One Minute Millionaire: The Enlightened Way to Wealth

30. Mayor Rudy Giuliani

Born in 1944 in Brooklyn, New York, USA

Occupation: attorney, consultant

Claim to Fame: mayor of New York City during the 9/11 attacks

Obstacles Faced: devastating attacks to his city on his watch, a bout with cancer in 2000

Achievements: prior to 9/11, he was the New York mayor who turned the city around; once notorious around the world for its dangerous streets, New York was recognized by the FBI as the safest large city in America, largely due to Giuliani's efforts; during and after 9/11, he became a symbol of exceptional leadership, gaining worldwide recognition and respect; called "America's Mayor"; named *Time* magazine's Person of the Year for 2001; given an honorary knighthood by Elizabeth II of the United Kingdom on 2002

Family: two children, Andrew and Caroline, with former wife Donna Hanover; married Judith Nathan in May 2003

Story: Following a career as a successful district attorney, Giuliani became the first Republican mayor of New York City in 20 years in 1993. The 107th mayor of New York City was re-elected in 1997, with a large majority.

With his final term as mayor drawing to an end, the infamous 9/11 terrorist attacks changed the world and offered a dark opportunity for true leadership to come to the fore. Giuliani's unwavering strength and effort as mayor calmed a terrified city and have been praised the world over.

He planned to run for New York State senator against Democrat Hillary Rodham Clinton. However, Giuliani announced his withdrawal from the senatorial race after he was diagnosed with the early stages of prostate cancer in April 2000.

A staunch Republican, Giuliani is known for some liberal views; pro-gun control and pro-choice, which are both admired and questioned. But his strength of character and heroism remain unquestionable. Many think he's a likely GOP candidate for president in 2008.

www.askmen.com

www.nyc.gov/html/rwg/html/bio.html

Leadership

Rudy Giuliani: Emperor of the City

31. Governor Arnold Schwarzenegger

Born in 1947 in Graz, Austria

Occupation: former bodybuilder, former actor, currently 38th governor of California

Obstacles Faced: his dreams seemed impossible to achieve; he could barely speak English when he came to the U.S.

Achievements: Golden Globe for Best Male Acting Debut; NATO International Star of the Year Award, 1984; NATO Male Star of the Year, 1987; MTV Movie Award for Best Male Performance, *Terminator 2: Judgment Day*; ShoWest: Humanitarian of the Year in 1997; seven Mr. Olympia titles

Family: married to journalist Maria Shriver, with four children

Story: The likelihood of an Austrian bodybuilder becoming an American governor would have been laughable before we were introduced to the force named Arnold Schwarzenegger. Today, we take him seriously.

First, he broke bodybuilding records and put the sport on the mainstream radar. With an unprecedented six consecutive Mr. Olympia titles and a seventh a few years later, he conquered the field. Then he set his sights on Hollywood. He conquered there, as well. He is one of the biggest movie stars of all time, with starring roles in *Total Recall, True Lies* and the *Terminator* movies.

Finally, he turned his powerful focus to politics. Arnold went on *The Tonight Show* to announce his candidacy for governor of California in August 2003. The world chuckled. Two months later, Schwarzenegger was elected as the 38th governor of California, earning 3.4 million votes. The world sat up and took notice.

He is a living symbol of the American Dream. His longtime marriage to Maria Shriver is respected as one of the strongest unions in politics and in Hollywood. Schwarzenegger has always been a force to be reckoned with, due to much more than his physical strength.

www.eonline.com/Facts/People/Bio/0,128,85,00.html

www.askmen.com

www.schwarzenegger.com/en/index.asp

www.governor.ca.gov/state/govsite/gov_homepage.jsp

Arnold Schwarzenegger (A&E Biography)

Why Arnold Matters: The Rise of a Cultural Icon

32. Dr. Condoleeza Rice

Born in 1954 in Birmingham, Alabama, USA

Occupation: U.S. national security advisor

Claim to Fame: first woman to occupy the post of national security advisor

Obstacles Faced: educated in the age of segregation

Achievements: an African-American woman in the American president's circle of influence; 1984 Walter J. Gores Award for Excellence in Teaching and the 1993 School of Humanities and Sciences Dean's Award for Distinguished Teaching; awarded honorary doctorates from Morehouse College, University of Alabama, University of Notre Dame, Mississippi College School of Law, the University of Louisville and Michigan State University

Story: Dr. Condoleeza Rice was named the Assistant to the President for National Security Affairs, commonly referred to as the National Security Advisor, on January 22, 2001. As a woman in that position and an African American, the achievement was significant. However, nobody could know just how significant national security was to become eight short months later. Fortunately, a strong and capable individual was at the helm.

Dr. Rice holds a bachelor's degree in political science from the University of Denver, her master's from the University of Notre Dame and her Ph.D. from the Graduate School of International Studies at the University of Denver. She is a Fellow of the American Academy of Arts and Sciences. As professor of political science, Dr. Rice has been on the Stanford faculty since 1981.

Rice has the ear of the leader of the free world. She is also a pianist, ice skater and sports fan.

www.whitehouse.gov/nsc/ricebio.html
Condi: The Condoleezza Rice Story
Condoleeza Rice: Being the Best

33. Michael Jordan

Born in 1963 in Brooklyn, New York, USA

Occupation: basketball champion, baseball team owner

Claim to Fame: best-known athlete in the world and the top basketball player ever

Obstacles Faced: the low odds of becoming an NBA champion

Achievements: his record-breaking achievements on the basketball court are matched by his commitment to children and family charitable causes; the first player to earn NBA's MVP award four times

Family: married, with two sons and a daughter

Story: With a basketball scholarship from the University of North Carolina, Michael Jordan scored his way onto the scene with the winning basket in the 1982 NCAA championship game. In 1984, Jordan led the United States basketball team to a gold medal at the Olympic Games in Los Angeles.

Jordan left college in 1984 to play with the Chicago Bulls. He finished his first season as one of the top scorers in the league and was named rookie of the year.

In 1987, he became the second player, after Wilt Chamberlain, to score more than 3,000 points in a single season. He led the NBA in scoring for seven consecutive seasons. He also became the Chicago Bulls' all-time leading scorer and set numerous scoring records. He led the Chicago Bulls to the NBA championship title in 1991, 1992 and 1993.

Jordan was also a member of the United States Olympic basketball team, known as the Dream Team, that captured the gold medal at the 1992 Olympics.

He's involved with numerous charities, including the Boys & Girls Club of America, UNCF/College Fund and Special Olympics. Jordan is a member of the board of America's Promise and is involved with the United Negro College Fund and the Make-A-Wish Foundation. In 1996, he opened the Jordan Institute for Families, which is designed to strengthen families.

www.jordan.sportsline.com

www.nba.com/playerfile/michael_jordan/bio.html

How to Be Like Mike: Life Lessons about Basketball's Best

I Can't Accept Not Trying: Michael Jordan on the Pursuit of Excellence

34. Robert Kiyosaki

Born in 1947 in Hawaii, USA

Occupation: businessman and author

Claim to Fame: teaches average Joes and Janes the techniques and principles of the wealthy

Obstacles Faced: poverty, bankruptcy, homelessness

Achievements: overcoming adversity to succeed and then sharing his strategies with the world

Family: married to Kim Kiyosaki

Story: Robert Kiyosaki had a unique education in wealth creation. Now he shares it worldwide with his lectures, books and even a popular board game. Already an entrepreneurial success with his innovative nylon and Velcro "surfer" wallets, Kiyosaki decided to offer what he knew to the world so that everyone with a desire for escaping the wage-slave trap could do so. Basically, he took the "secrets" of the rich public.

In 1985, Robert founded an education company that taught business and investing to tens of thousands of individuals across the planet. Retiring at the age of 47, he wrote *Rich Dad, Poor Dad*, a #1 New York Times best seller.

Riding the wave of the book's amazing popularity and appeal, he went on to create the patented board game Cashflow® 101. The game teaches people the same financial principles that he learned as a youth and wrote about in his book. The Rich Dad series of books and resources make financial concepts accessible and straightforward. *Rich Dad, Poor Dad* is distinguished by being on the Forbes "20 Most Influential Business Books" list.

Kiyosaki not only invites us to create financial change but a mental change as well.

www.richdad.com

Rich Dad, Poor Dad: What the Rich Teach Their Kids About Money—That the Poor and Middle Class Do Not!

Cashflow Quadrant: Rich Dad's Guide to Financial Freedom

35. Mel Gibson

Born in 1956 in Peekskill, New York, USA

Occupation: actor, movie producer, director

Claim to Fame: movie star with talent, passion and drive

Obstacles Faced: Gibson reportedly hit bottom in the 90's; dealing with addictions at this dark time, he has said his life was depleted of spirituality and "I just didn't want to go on"

Achievements: starring in, producing and directing some of the best films of our age, multiple Oscars, Golden Globes, People's Choice awards and many international awards

Family: Gibson and his wife of 24 years, Robyn, have seven children

Story: Although born in America, Mel Gibson moved with his large family—he is the sixth of eleven children—to New South Wales, Australia. While building a good reputation in Australia by acting in small productions, he earned an award for Best Actor from the Australian Film Institute, the equivalent to the Oscar, for his role in *Tim* in 1979. However, that same year, it was the original *Mad Max* movie that made him known worldwide.

Garnering more awards and recognition for his next several roles, 1995 brought his most famous role as Sir William Wallace in *Braveheart*, for which he won two Oscars for Best Picture and Best Director.

With more than 50 movie credits and various awards behind him (Golden Globes, People's Choice, etc.), Gibson completed a groundbreaking and controversial project in 2004 that set him apart from all other celebrity actors. *The Passion of The Christ* is a vivid depiction of the last 12 hours of Jesus Christ's life, written, produced and directed by Gibson. In fact, he reportedly financed the film out of his own pocket for about $30 million.

According to Gibson, it was facing a foreboding sense of "spiritual bankruptcy" in the early 1990's that led him to reexamine his faith and ultimately to create *The Passion.*

www.melgibson.com

www.thepassionofthechrist.com/splash.htm

Mel Gibson: Man on a Mission

Mel Gibson's Passion and Philosophy: The Cross, the Questions, the Controversy

36. Steve Jobs

Born in 1955 in San Francisco, California, USA

Occupation: CEO of Apple and Pixar

Claim to Fame: co-founder of Apple and Pixar

Obstacles Faced: in July 2004, Jobs had a surgical operation to remove a cancerous tumor in his pancreas; it was a very rare form of pancreatic cancer

Achievements: sparked the personal computer revolution in the 1970s with the Apple, and reinvented the personal computer in the 1980s with the Macintosh; both Apple and Pixar are distinguished with many awards for their respective innovation and leadership

Family: married, with four children

Story: In 1976, Steve Jobs and his friend Steve Wozniak founded Apple Computers in the Jobs' family garage. At the time, Jobs was 21. Today he's the CEO of Apple and the CEO of Pixar, the Academy-Award-winning animation studios which he co-founded in 1986.

Apple creates some of the best personal computers in the world and is widely regarded as being of the most innovative in the industry. Pixar has created five of the most successful animated movies of all time: *Toy Story* (1995); *A Bug's Life* (1998); *Toy Story 2* (1999); *Monsters, Inc.* (2001); and *Finding Nemo* (2003). Pixar's five films have earned multiple awards and more than $2 billion at the box office.

Jobs is one of the most famous people in the personal computer industry. Jobs is ranked in the *Guinness Book of World Records* as the lowest-paid CEO for his annual salary of $1. But he does alright with his 10-million-share options of the company, in addition to his earnings from Pixar.

www.apple.com/pr/bios/jobs.html
www.en.wikipedia.org/wiki/Steve_Jobs
Steve Jobs: Thinks Different
The Second Coming of Steve Jobs

37. Muhammad Ali

Born in 1942 in Kentucky, USA

Occupation: boxing champion

Claim to Fame: three-time Heavyweight Champion of the World

Obstacles Faced: racism, imprisoned for his beliefs, Parkinson's disease

Achievements: of 61 fights, he won 56, 37 by KO; he lost only 5, 1 by KO; named Sportsman of the Century by *Sports Illustrated*

Family: married to Yolanda, with nine children

Story: Cassius Marcellus Clay, Jr. was a child destined for greatness, although the road was often rocky. A prize-winning boxer in his youth, Ali became an Olympic Gold medalist in the 1960 Rome Olympics. He was 18 years old. His legendary confidence was sparked by his now-famous claim of his own ability to "float like a butterfly, sting like a bee."

Not long after his championship, Clay began to make a difference on both political and racial fronts. Dismayed by the prevalent racism towards African Americans in his own country, he protested by ceremoniously throwing his Olympic gold medal into a river. In 1964, he converted to Islam and was given the name that's gone down in history, Muhammad Ali.

In 1967, he refused to be drafted in protest to the Vietnam War. In response, the World Boxing Association took away his boxing license and his title. He was sentenced to five years in prison for violating the Selective Service Act.

Released from prison on appeal, Ali returned to boxing to make his mark with an astonishing record and a famous comeback.

Just three years after his retirement, Ali was diagnosed in 1982 with Parkinson's disease. Years later, we witnessed his physical deterioration—as well as his fierce pride and determination—when he was honored by lighting the Olympic torch at the 1996 Olympic Games in Atlanta.

www.espn.go.com/classic/biography/s/Ali_Muhammad.html

www.muhammad-ali.info

King of the World

Muhammad Ali

The Greatest

38. Queen Elizabeth II

Born in 1926 to the British Royal Family

Occupation: monarch of the Commonwealth and the United Kingdom's head of state

Claim to Fame: now in her late seventies, The Queen continues working the full-time job she has held for more than 50 years

Obstacles Faced: wars, economic recessions, parliamentary upheavals, family problems, constitutional challenges, declining interest in the monarchy

Achievements: maintaining a leadership of strength, consistency and grace during a tumultuous period in the history of Britain and the world; The Queen does not receive awards, she gives them

Family: The Queen and her husband the Duke of Edinborough have four children: Prince Charles, now The Prince of Wales; Princess Anne, now The Princess Royal; Prince Andrew, now The Duke of York and Prince Edward, now The Earl of Wessex

Story: The coronation of 26-year-old Elizabeth took place on June 2, 1953, after the death of her father, King George VI. Her Majesty has a significant role in every branch of government. For instance, she is the head of the armed forces, and only she can declare war. She cannot, however, exercise this power without the advice of her ministers. As Sovereign, Her Majesty is head of the Navy, Army and Air Force of Britain.

The Queen is Patron or President of over 700 organizations. Each year she undertakes a large number of engagements. For example, in 2003 she presided at 478 ceremonies and events throughout the world. In 2002, the 50th year of her reign, she celebrated her Golden Jubilee. Despite a growing sense of the declining relevance of the monarchy, Queen Elizabeth remains one of the world's most popular and respected leaders.

www.canadianheritage.gc.ca/special/jubilee/e-biography.htm
www.royalty.nu/Europe/England/Windsor/ElizabethII.html
www.royal.gov.uk/output/Page1.asp
Queen Elizabeth II: A Celebration of Her Majesty's Fifty-Year Reign
Lilibet: An Intimate Portrait of Elizabeth II

39. Bono

Born in 1960 in Dublin, Ireland

Occupation: rock star, humanitarian

Claim to Fame: lead singer, songwriter of the group U2

Obstacles Faced: faced a personal tragedy when his mother died of a brain aneurysm while attending the funeral of her own father, when Bono was 15

Achievements: raises funds for drought, famine and AIDS in Africa; included on the 2002 List of "100 Greatest Britons"; earned the title "Most Powerful Man in Music" by Q magazine in 2002

Family: married, with four children

Story: Born an average Dubliner, Paul David Hewson followed his passion for music and truth into music stardom as lead singer of the mega-band U2. Originally cast as a 'Christian-rock' band from Ireland, U2 has overcome borders and labels.

With one of the most successful evolutions in rock history and a long list of hits, U2 is just one way that Bono speaks his message of peace, justice and truth. Beyond U2, Bono has emerged as a political and social activist. Since 1999, he's become increasingly involved in campaigning for third-world debt relief and the plight of Africa.

In 1999, Bono attended the G8 Summit in Germany, met with Pope John Paul II and participated in the NetAid concert at America's Millennium Gala. He also met with U.S. President George W. Bush to further his case for African relief. A rock star with the respect of world leaders, he counts as friends and allies prime ministers, presidents, UN top officials, religious leaders and activists.

Bono is the co-founder of Debt, Aids, Trade in Africa (DATA), an organization that raises awareness about Africa's unpayable debts, uncontrolled spread of AIDS and unfair trade rules that hurt the countries' poor citizens.

www.u2.com

www.en.wikipedia.org/wiki/Bono

www.time.com/time/covers/1101020304/story.html

www.data.org

Bono: His Life, Music, and Passions

Walk On: The Spiritual Journey of U2

40. Brian Tracy

Born in Canada and raised in California, USA

Occupation: author, speaker, coach, mentor

Achievements: addresses more than 500,000 men and women each year on the subjects of personal and professional development, traveled and worked in over 85 countries and speaks four languages

Family: wife Barbara, with four children

Story: As one of America's leading authorities on the development of human potential and personal effectiveness, Brian Tracy has produced more than 300 different audio and video learning programs, covering the entire spectrum of human and corporate performance over the past 25 years.

Before becoming the guru he is considered today, Tracy had successful careers in sales and marketing, investments and real estate development. He decided to follow his passion, and he found his niche a global audience of individuals clamoring for information and education in self-development.

As the best-selling author of 17 books, Tracy is well known to publishers, on the speaker's circuit and on the Internet. He is the chairman of Brian Tracy International, a human resource company, whose team extends throughout 31 countries.

www.briantracy.com

www.tracyint.com

Many Miles to Go

Change Your Thinking, Change Your Life:
How to Unlock Your Full Potential for Success and Achievement

Million Dollar Habits

Create Your Own Future: How to Master the 12 Critical Factors of Unlimited Success

41. Christopher Reeve

Born in 1952 in New York City, USA; sadly, Christopher Reeve passed away on October 10th, 2004, prior to this book being published

Occupation: actor, director, activist

Claim to Fame: transcended disability

Obstacles Faced: suffered a spinal cord injury at the top of his game, which left him unable to move and breathe on his own

Achievements: has advanced the cause of finding treatments and a cure for paralysis caused by spinal cord injury and other central nervous system disorders; in September 2003, Reeve was awarded the Mary Woodard Lasker Award for Public Service in Support of Medical Research and the Health Sciences from the Lasker Foundation

Family: married to Dana, with three children

Story: He started acting as a teenager and earned the reputation as one of the country's leading actors by the time he was 25. Christopher Reeve will forever be known as Superman, from the series of movies in which he portrayed the superhero. Maybe that's why it stunned us so much when he was suddenly paralyzed by a fall during an equestrian competition in 1995.

Reeve's incredible story of survival, love and determination has inspired millions to look beyond the surface and see the strength in all people, despite disability. His books, *Still Me* and *Nothing Is Impossible*, describe his struggle with, acceptance and transcendence of his tragedy. Reeve has put a human face on spinal cord injury and has brought awareness to the mainstream. In doing so, he's motivated neuroscientists around the world to better understand the complex diseases of the brain and central nervous system.

His love for acting overcame his paralysis, and he produced and starred in a major television movie from his wheelchair. The updated version of the classic Hitchcock thriller *Rear Window* won him a Golden Globe Award nomination and the Screen Actors Guild Award for Best Actor in a Television Movie or Miniseries.

www.christopherreeve.org

www.paralysis.org

Christopher Reeve (A & E Biography)

Nothing is Impossible: Reflections on a New Life

42. Lance Armstrong

Born in 1971 in Dallas, Texas, USA

Occupation: champion cyclist, activist

Claim to Fame: overcame cancer to win the Tour de France a record six times

Obstacles Faced: cancer

Achievements: besides being an inspiration to the world, has raised hundreds of millions of dollars for cancer research

Family: divorced, with two children

Story: In 1999, a cyclist stood among many at the starting line of the Tour de France, the world's most renowned bicycle race of 3,500 kilometers. Although a relative unknown at the time, this cyclist was already a winner, and the race was already a victory—both for him and for cancer survivors everywhere. He had beaten the odds and conquered a deadly form of cancer. That fact alone made it astonishing that he was even a contender in the race. He won the race. It was official: Lance Armstrong was an international hero.

What an inspiring story, even if it ended there. But it doesn't. Armstrong also won the Tour de France the following year—and then the next. Unbelievably, Lance Armstrong overcame cancer to win the grueling race six years running, including the 2004 Tour on July 25th.

At age 25, Lance was diagnosed with advanced testicular cancer that had spread to his lungs and his brain and given a 50-50 chance of recovery. With leading-edge treatment and singular determination, he beat the disease. He didn't just survive; he conquered.

The degree of his championship after such an obstacle seems almost unfathomable. Awarded virtually every sports honor there is, he is a worldwide icon of hope. He also continues to be a leader and activist on behalf of cancer survivors around the world.

www.tourofhope.org/index.htm
www.laf.org
It's Not About the Bike
Every Second Counts

43. Madonna

Born in 1958 in Michigan, USA

Occupation: performer, songwriter, actor, producer

Claim to Fame: pop icon

Obstacles Faced: lost her mother to breast cancer at the age of five

Achievements: won a Golden Globe for Best Actress for her starring role in 1995's *Evita,* has had over 25 top ten singles

Family: married to director Guy Ritchie, with two children—one from a previous relationship

Story: Over the last 20 years, Madonna has sold close to two hundred million albums worldwide. Born Madonna Louise Veronica Ciccone, she relocated to New York City in 1977 in order to pursue her dream of becoming a world famous ballet dancer. As we know, she did achieve international fame for her artistic abilities, but it was her music and her self-styled persona that launched her to super-stardom.

In 1983 and '84, with the releases of hits "Holiday" and "Borderline," Madonna literally rocketed to stardom. Her blend of music, style and attitude hit a nerve with a generation, and she shrewdly positioned herself at the crest of a giant demographic wave. Madonna's ability of sensing emerging trends and then leading them to the mainstream, has earned her the reputation as an excellent business woman and trend-setter.

In the mid-eighties, at the height of her "Material Girl" popularity, Madonna ventured into movies by starring in Susan Seidelman's *Desperately Seeking Susan,* which achieved a measure of critical success. It wasn't until 1995, though, that she landed the coveted title role in an adaptation of Andrew Lloyd Webber's *Evita.* She won a Golden Globe and added 'actor' to her list of credits.

Now, married with children and five best-selling children's books to her name.

www.biography.com/search/article.jsp?aid=9394994

www.home.madonna.com

Madonna As Postmodern Myth: How One Star's Self-Construction Rewrites Sex, Gender, Hollywood and the American Dream

The English Roses

44. Sir Paul McCartney

Born in 1942 in Liverpool, England

Occupation: musician, performer, humanitarian, legend

Claim to Fame: one quarter of The Beatles—the biggest musical group ever

Obstacles Faced: death of first wife Linda from breast cancer

Achievements: in 1997, Paul McCartney was knighted by The Queen for his services to music; multiple humanitarian honors; honored by PETA (along with Linda) for his work in animal rights; numerous professional awards; inducted into the Rock & Roll Hall of Fame as a solo artist in 1999; voted "The Composer of the Millennium" by a BBC poll; knighted in 1997 at Buckingham Palace

Family: now married to Heather Mills McCartney, with four children—three from his first marriage of 30 years to Linda McCartney, who died of breast cancer

Story: Paul McCartney, along with three other working-class lads from Liverpool, became the musical and cultural phenomenon we loved—The Beatles. Instantly recognizable to most of us, the music of The Beatles now forms a part of the foundation of our cultural history. With record-breaking sales and smash hits too numerous to name, "Beatlemania" took over the world and gave an entire generation a soundtrack.

The Beatles disbanded in 1971, after the release of *Let It Be*—the album, film and single. But Paul McCartney's star didn't stop rising. Today he's one of the richest men in Europe and certainly one of the most famous, respected and beloved.

After The Beatles, he founded the band *Wings* with his wife Linda. That followed with decades of superior solo work. In his sixties, he still instantly draws a crowd and continues to give them the lyrics, tunes and familiar vocals they want.

An active humanitarian, McCartney contributes much of his time, attention and resources to charitable work.

www.paulmccartney.com
www.thebeatles.com
www.askmen.com/men/entertainment/49_paul_mccartney.html
Each One Believing: on Stage, off Stage, and Backstage
Paul McCartney: Now and Then

45. Paul Newman

Born in 1925 in Ohio, USA

Occupation: actor, philanthropist

Claim to Fame: appeared in over 60 films; with his "Newman's Own" line of food products, has donated more than $100 million to charities

Obstacles Faced: son died of an accidental drug overdose in 1978

Achievements: iconic movie star who turned his energies to charity; in 1992 Newman and his wife were recognized at the prestigious Kennedy Center Honors for their philanthropic endeavors

Family: married for 46 years to Joanne Woodward, with three daughters and a son, who passed away in 1978

Story: The blue-eyed Paul Newman had an active life before the fame of his blockbuster movie star years. He served in the Navy during World War II, after transferring from the Air Force due to color blindness. After his stint in the Navy, he earned a degree in literature and acting in 1949. The usual struggle for an amateur actor ended in 1958, the year Newman received an Oscar nomination (his first) for his role in *Cat On a Hot Tin Roof.* He married Joanne Woodward that same year.

Nominated for the Oscar six more times for his role in films, which included *The Hustler, Hud* and *Cool Hand Luke.* He eventually won the Oscar in 1987 for his part in *The Color of Money.*

Today Newman's time and attention is focused on his charitable work. The profits from his "Newman's Own" line of salad dressings and other food products are donated to charitable organizations, such as, The Hole in the Wall Gang Camp for terminally ill children and the Scott Newman Foundation for drug and alcohol abuse education. The Newmans also provide funds for drought relief in Africa.

www.tiscali.co.uk/entertainment/film/biographies/paul_newman_biog.html

www.amctv.com/article/0,,1086-1--0-9-EST,00.html

Shameless Exploitation in Pursuit of the Common Good: The Madcap Business Adventure by the Truly Oddest Couple

The Newman's Own Organics Guide to a Good Life: Simple Measures That Benefit You and the Place You Live

46. Robert Allen

Born in Camden, New Jersey, USA

Occupation: success coach, speaker, author

Claim to Fame: has succeeded by helping others to succeed

Achievements: author of *Nothing Down* and *The One Minute Millionaire*

Story: Robert Allen is the author of one of the largest-selling financial books in history. A *New York Times* best seller *Nothing Down* established Allen as one of the most influential investment advisors ever, while effectively launching the financial success of millions of ordinary people. It's very possible that Robert Allen can be credited with making more millionaires than anyone else in history.

Allen's other books and programs include *The Road to Wealth* and *Multiple Streams of Income*, which continue to bring the strategies and tactics of the very wealthy to a mainstream audience. Thousands of people have attended his cutting-edge investment seminars over the past 20 years.

A popular talk-show guest, Allen has appeared on hundreds of programs, including *Good Morning America* and *Larry King Live*. He has also been featured in the *Wall Street Journal, Newsweek, Barron's, Money Magazine* and *Reader's Digest*.

In 2002, he collaborated with Mark Victor Hansen (of the Chicken Soup series) and wrote *The One Minute Millionaire*, a book that breaks new ground in the world of financial success. The book presents the concept of the enlightened millionaire—one who balances wealth and abundance with spiritual principles and a connection with the universal principle of abundance. Tapping into a new wave of people who no longer want wealth for wealth's sake, Allen and Hansen have helped to redefine what it is to be rich.

The world is shifting in so many ways, even financially. Building wealth today is not what it once was. Robert Allen has identified this shift, mapped the new financial landscape and shared his findings with the world.

 www.multiplestreamsofincome.com
One Minute Millionaire (free with CD)
Multiple Streams of Income
Creating Wealth

47. Prime Minister Tony Blair

Born in 1953 in Edinburgh, Scotland

Occupation: prime minister of Great Britain

Obstacles Faced: terrorism

Achievements: prime minister of Great Britain, longest-sitting labour prime minister of the U.K.

Family: married to Cherie Booth, one of Britain's most prominent lawyers, with four children; youngest son is the first child born to a sitting prime minister in over 150 years

Story: In England in 1997, The Labour Party won the General Election by a landslide, after 18 years in opposition. At the age of 43, Tony Blair became the youngest prime minister of Britain since 1812.

Blair launched his dramatic strategy to restructure the Labour Party and its platform to bring its traditional goals more in line with the majority of British citizens. His government implemented a far-reaching program of constitutional change, with Blair's priorities on education, public services and the National Health Service.

Very popular, Mr. Blair was re-elected with another landslide majority in 2001. Like so many world leaders, since September 11, 2001, his agenda has been dominated by the "War on Terror" and Britain's involvement in the Iraq War. As one of America's strongest allies, Prime Minister Blair navigates the country through very difficult and dangerous times.

www.number-10.gov.uk

Tony Blair by Philip Stephens

Tony Blair by John Rentoul

Thirty Days

48. Barbara Walters

Born in 1931 in Boston, Massachusetts, USA

Occupation: journalist, TV anchor person

Claim to Fame: the alpha female of broadcast news

Achievements: induction into the Academy of Television Arts and Sciences' Hall of Fame "for being acknowledged worldwide as one of television's most respected interviewers and journalists" (1990); five Emmy awards; National Association of Television Program Executives Award; International Radio and Television Society, Broadcaster of the Year Award; Overseas Press Club, President's Award; George Foster Peabody Award for one-on-one interview with paralyzed actor Christopher Reeve; Lifetime Achievement Award, International Women's Media Foundation; Lifetime Achievement Award, Women's Project and Productions; Lifetime Achievement Award, National Academy of Television Arts and Sciences

Family: divorced, with one daughter

Story: Barbara Walters was the first woman to anchor the network nightly news when she signed with ABC in 1976, during an era where women simply didn't break through the glass ceiling like that.

In 1979, she became a correspondent for *20/20* and eventually became its co-anchor, a position that has been uniquely hers since 1984. Her other television work includes award-winners *The Barbara Walters Show* and *The View.*

In 1999, Ms. Walters conducted the first interview with Monica Lewinsky, which proved to be the highest-rated news program ever broadcast by a single network. Another of her famous "firsts" was an hour-long primetime conversation with Cuban President Fidel Castro. Walters also conducted the first-ever interview for American television with Russia's President Vladimir Putin and the first interview with President and Mrs. Bush following September 11th.

Virtually every big name in the news has sat down and answered questions by Barbara Walters. She invariably asks the tough questions—the ones we all want answered.

www.abcnews.go.com/sections/2020/2020/barbara_walters_bio.html
www.en.wikipedia.org/wiki/Barbara_Walters
www.abc.go.com/theview/hosts/walters.html
How to Talk With Practically Anybody About Practically Anything

49. Marianne Williamson

Born in 1952 in Houston, Texas, USA

Occupation: author, lecturer, peace activist

Claim to Fame: leader of The Church of Today; popular writer and speaker on spirituality

Key Achievements: advocates for the need for greater tolerance, compassion and spiritual awareness globally, locally, politically and individually

Story: Marianne Williamson's words inspire us, challenge us and help us to see more clearly. Four of her books, including the mega best-seller *A Return to Love* and the newly-released *Everyday Grace*, have been #1 *New York Times* best sellers. She writes about what it is to be human, to be a modern woman, to be an American. She writes and lectures on the possibilities for our future.

When *A Return to Love* was released in 1992, it became a publishing sensation, topping the *New York Times* best-seller list for over half a year, smashing several publishing records and establishing Williamson as one of today's most prominent spiritual figures.

As one of America's most visionary thinkers, her projects always place emphasis on spirituality. A popular guest on television shows such as *Oprah, Larry King Live* and *Good Morning America*, Williamson also maintains a full schedule of lecturing around the world, which she has done for the past 20 years.

In 1989, she founded Project Angel Food, a meals-on-wheels program that serves homebound people with AIDS in the Los Angeles area. Today Project Angel Food serves over 1,000 people daily. She co-founded the Global Renaissance Alliance, a worldwide network of peace activists. The organization's mission is to harness the power of non-violence as a social force for good.

Williamson is the spiritual leader of The Church of Today, one of the largest and fastest growing New Thought churches in the United States, with a congregation of several thousand.

www.marianne.com

www.renaissanceunity.com

Everyday Grace: Having Hope, Finding Forgiveness, and Making Miracles
A Return to Love: Reflections on the Principles of "A Course in Miracles"
Woman's Worth

50. Michael Dell

Born in 1965 in Houston, Texas, USA

Occupation: chairman and CEO of the fastest-growing major computer systems business in the world—Dell Computer Corporation

Claim to Fame: Dell is widely recognized as one of the top vendors of personal computers worldwide

Obstacles Faced: started out with $1,000 capital in an industry dominated by giant corporations

Achievements: *The Wall Street Journal* named Dell Computers number one in total returns to investors over the past three, five and ten years; earned the titles of "Entrepreneur of the Year" from *Inc.* magazine, "Man of the Year" by *PC* magazine, "Top CEO in American Business" from *Worth* magazine and "CEO of the Year" by *Financial World* and *Industry Week* magazines

Family: married

Story: Michael Dell founded the Dell Computer Corporation in 1984 with $1,000 and an idea. The company is now worth billions because of Dell's instinct to eliminate the middleman and sell custom-built personal computers directly to the consumers.

Dell built an empire out of nothing in 15 years. He created wealth for millions of people. Dell Computers' revenues exceed $23 billion. Dell has sales offices in over 34 countries and more than 33,000 employees in over 170 countries. It's the largest online commercial seller of computer systems with an average of over $30 million per day in online sales. Mr. Dell is the youngest CEO of a company ever to earn a ranking on the Fortune 500. Dell is currently the only company on the list whose revenues have increased by over 40% annually for the past three consecutive years.

The company is loved by its loyal (and ever-expanding) consumer base and for their delivery of exceptional support and customer service. The value of Dell's stock has risen 70,000% over the past decade. His leadership style is considered leading-edge and has earned him several awards of recognition.

www.askmen.com/men/january00/8_michael_dell.html
www.infoplease.com/ipa/A0763659.html
www.dell.com
Direct from Dell: Strategies that Revolutionized an Industry

51. Dr. Robert Schuller

Born in 1926 in Iowa, USA

Occupation: American protestant minister and television evangelist

Claim to Fame: possibly one of most listened-to orators in the world

Achievements: received the Horatio Alger Award; Freedom Foundation Awards; Clergyman of the Year, presented by Religious Heritage of America; Awards of Excellence for Religion in Media; Peacemaker Awards

Family: married, with five children

Story: Dr. Robert A. Schuller is watched by over ten million TV viewers around the world daily, as the host of *The Hour of Power*. Dr. Schuller is the author of more than 30 books, including five which have been on the *New York Times* best-sellers list.

From humble beginnings in the world of ministry, Schuller has built, at the urging of his congregations, a Protestant empire. Starting out in the early 1950's with his wife as organist and $500 in assets, he rented a drive-in theater and conducted Sunday services from the roof of the snack bar.

Today his Reformed Church in America congregation is housed in a multi-million-dollar edifice in southern California called the Crystal Cathedral. This 2,736-seat edifice is visited by a million worshippers a year, for regular Sunday worship, for conferences, seminars, workshops and for two annual pageants, *The Glory of Christmas* and *The Glory of Easter*.

www.faith.premierespeakers.com/1808/index.cfm
Hours of Power: My Daily Book of Motivation and Inspiration
Success Is Never Ending, Failure Is Never Final

52. Stephen King

Born in 1947 in Maine, USA

Occupation: author, director, producer

Claim to Fame: as prolific and popular a writer as Shakespeare was in his time

Obstacles Faced: his father abandoned his family when Stephen was a young child, alcohol and drug addictions, seriously injured by a hit-and-run driver

Achievements: frightening, fascinating and compelling his readers since the 1960's, 2003 recipient of *The National Book Foundation Medal for Distinguished Contribution to American Letters,* National Book Award for lifetime achievement in 2003

Family: married to author Tabitha King

Story: Ever sat up past your bedtime reading a Stephen King novel? Tens of millions of us have. His books (and subsequent movies) are considered milestones in North American culture: *The Shining, Carrie, Firestarter, Dead Zone, Misery, The Green Mile,* to name but a handful. Since 1976, King has authored (or directed or produced) 82 works.

Once a high school teacher in Maine, King is now the king of his genre. His books have been translated into 33 different languages and published in over 35 different countries. There are over 300 million copies of his novels in publication.

The Kings provide scholarships for local high school students and contribute to many other local and national charities.

www.stephenking.com/index_flash.php

www.utopianweb.com/king/bio.asp

On Writing

Carrie

The Dark Tower series

The Stand

Tommyknockers

Needful Things

53. Senator John McCain

Born in 1936 in the Panama Canal Zone

Occupation: senior senator from Arizona; chairman of the Senate Committee on Commerce, Science and Transportation; also serves on the Armed Services and Indian Affairs Committees

Claim to Fame: crosses partisan boundaries with a unique blend of conservatism on military and social issues and liberalism on fiscal issues

Obstacles Faced: solitary confinement as a prisoner of war in North Vietnam

Achievements: the nation's foremost leader in national defense and foreign policy matters; numerous awards, in addition to the Paul H. Douglas Ethics in Government award, which he received with Senator Russ Feingold for his efforts at campaign finance reform; named one of the "25 Most Influential People in America" by *Time* magazine in 1997

Family: married, with seven children and four grandchildren

Story: A Naval Academy graduate, John McCain is distinguished by a 22-year career as a naval aviator. In 1967, he was shot down over Vietnam and held as a prisoner of war in Hanoi for five-and-a-half years (1967-1973), much of it in solitary confinement.

McCain's naval honors include the Silver Star, Bronze Star, Legion of Merit, Purple Heart and Distinguished Flying Cross. He retired from the Navy as a captain in 1981 and stepped into a highly successful career in politics.

In 1982, he was elected to Congress and in 1986 elected to the U.S senate. McCain ran unsuccessfully for the Republican nomination for president of the United States in 2000. He is widely considered as a possibility for president in 2008.

www.mccain.senate.gov

John McCain: An American Odyssey

Man of the People: The Life of John McCain

Faith of My Fathers

54. Tom Peters

Born in 1942 in Baltimore, Maryland, USA

Occupation: chairman of Tom Peters Company

Claim to Fame: considered the father of the post-modern corporation

Obstacles Faced: his unconventional business perspective compelled *Business Week* to describe him as "business' best friend and worst nightmare"

Achievements: co-authored (with Bob Waterman) *In Search of Excellence* in 1982—ranked as the "greatest business book of all time" in a 2002 poll by Britain's Bloomsbury Publishing; in 1999, it was named one of the "Top Three Business Books of the Century" by NPR; holds several honorary degrees, including from the State University of Management in Moscow, awarded in 2004

Family: Tom and his wife Susan Sargent reside on a 1,500-acre farm in Vermont with their two sons

Story: Described as a guru by *Fortune* and *The Economist*, Tom Peters has re-defined business management in the modern world. In order to map the new landscape, Peters tore up the old maps and tossed out the old paradigms, to much controversy and criticism.

His 1982 book *In Search of Excellence* has become a bible in the business world. Peters followed *Search*'s huge success with a string of other international best sellers. Most recently, in October 2003, he released *Re-imagine! Business Excellence in a Disruptive Age*. Already acknowledged as a revolutionary book, it was an immediate international best seller.

A graduate of Cornell and Stanford Universities, earning an MBA and Ph.D., Peters served two tours of active duty in Vietnam in the Navy. He also served as a senior White House drug abuse advisor in 1973.

In a study by Accenture's Institute for Strategic Change in 2002, Peters scored second among the top 50 Business Intellectuals, behind Michael Porter.

www.tompeters.com
Re-imagine!
The Pursuit of Wow!
In Search of Excellence

55. Bill Cosby

Born in 1937 in Philadelphia, Pennsylvania, USA

Occupation: comedian, director, producer

Claim to Fame: produced, wrote, directed and starred in *The Cosby Show*

Obstacles Faced: the death of his only son

Achievements: Cosby was awarded the Kennedy Center Honors in 1998 and the Presidential Medal of Freedom in 2002

Family: married to Camille Hanks, with four daughters; only son Ennis Cosby, aged 27, was murdered in 1997 in Los Angeles, California

Story: Bill Cosby has starred in 30 films and TV shows. He has produced, written and directed dozens of others, including the ground-breaking sitcom *The Cosby Show*, which portrayed for the first time a wealthy and stable African-American family.

Ever popular, Cosby has appeared on over 40 talk shows from Andy Williams, Dean Martin and Johnny Carson in the 1960's, to today's David Letterman and Ellen DeGeneres shows.

Cosby plays a unique role in the civil rights movement by advancing the status and equality of African Americans with a savvy combination of his shows, his success and his personality. In 1999 he won the People's Choice Award for All-Time Favorite Performer.

Not one to rest on his laurels, he raised a controversy in May 2004 at the National Association for Advancement of Colored People gala by pointing out the difference between today's MTV generation and the civil rights activists of the 1960's. He called on today's youth to focus less on style and materialism and more on substance and the fight for social equality.

www.en.wikipedia.org/wiki/Presidential_Medal_of_Freedom

www.en.wikipedia.org/wiki/Kennedy_Center_Honors

www.naacp.org

www.celebritywonder.com/html/billcosby.html

I Am What I Ate. . . and I'm Frightened!!! And Other Digressions from the Doctor of Comedy

Love and Marriage

Cosbyology: Essays and Observations From the Doctor of Comedy

56. J.K. Rowling

Born in 1966 in Chipping Sodbury, England

Occupation: author

Claim to Fame: creator of *Harry Potter*, the fastest-selling book series in history

Obstacles Faced: divorced and living on public assistance in a tiny apartment with her baby daughter, Rowling wrote *Harry Potter and the Sorcerer's Stone* in longhand during her daughter's naps

Achievements: the books are wildly popular; the fifth title, *Harry Potter and the Order of the Phoenix*, has broken records with its first print run of 6.8 million copies and a second print run of an additional 1.7 million copies, a figure unprecedented for any book, ever; won the Hugo Award, the Bram Stoker Award, the Whitbread Award for Best Children's Book and a special commendation for the Anne Spencer Lindbergh Prize as well as many other honors; named an Officer of the British Empire

Family: married, with two children

Story: Joanne Kathleen Rowling graduated from Exeter University and worked as a secretary and an English teacher. After her daughters birth, she needed a way to make ends meet; she wrote a children's story. In 1998, *Harry Potter and the Sorcerer's Stone* was published in the United States and Harry-mania was launched.

Today, with five books of the series published, there are 80 million copies in print in America alone and each title has been on *The New York Times, USA Today* and *Wall Street Journal* best-seller lists. Worldwide, there are over a quarter of a billion books sold. They've been translated into 61 languages and distributed in over 200 countries. All five books have appeared on best-seller lists internationally.

Rowling's level of popularity makes the standard bookstore readings impossible. Usually, a very popular author might draw several hundred fans to a well-promoted reading or signing. On the Canadian portion of her worldwide publicity tour, Rowling did only three readings: one in Toronto and two in Vancouver and all in venues reserved for sporting events and rock concerts. She read to almost 20,000 adoring fans on each occasion.

www.jkrowling.com
J.K. Rowling A Biography
Harry Potter and the Sorcerer's Stone

57. Anita Roddick

Born in 1942 in Littlehampton, England

Occupation: business owner, human-rights activist, patron for environmental, equal rights, education and health causes

Claim to Fame: in 1998, *The Financial Times* ranked The Body Shop the 27th most-respected company in the world

Obstacles Faced: building a business with no formal business training

Achievements: altered the landscape of old-world business with a mission of supporting environmental and humanitarian causes; Women's Business Development Center's First Annual Woman Power Award, USA; Women's Center's Leadership Award, USA; The Gleitsman Foundation's Award of Achievement, USA; United Nations Environment Programme (UNEP), Honouree, Eyes on the Environment; British Environment & Media Award; Dame Commander of the British Empire

Family: married, with two daughters

Story: Anita Roddick opened the first Body Shop in Brighton, Sussex, England in 1976. At the time, the budding entrepreneur had experience as a librarian, a teacher, a restaurant owner and in the United Nations' Women's Rights Department of the International Labor Organization. The Body Shop came from a need to create a livelihood for herself and her two daughters. Now, 32 years later, it's an award-winning, multi-national business with over 2,000 stores in 50 countries, serving 80 million customers in 25 languages.

The commercial strength of The Body Shop is born from the shared values that set it apart from mainstream businesses. An example of the company's work is their collaboration with a group of human-rights activists to free the American political prisoners known as the Angola Three. These three men, who were black political activists in the 1970s, have served over 31 years in solitary confinement in Angola prison for crimes they did not commit.

www.anitaroddick.com

www.myhero.com/myhero/hero.asp?hero=Roddick

Take It Personally: How to Make Conscious Choices to Change the World

A Revolution in Kindness

58. Barbra Streisand

Born in 1942 in New York City, USA

Occupation: singer, actor, producer, director

Claim to Fame: highest-selling female recording artist ever; has had number one albums in each of the last four decades

Achievements: only artist to earn Oscars, Tonys, Emmys, Grammys, Golden Globes, Cable Ace, Peabody and American Film Institute's Life Achievement Award; recognition for her involvement in charitable and social causes include the 1992 Commitment to Life Award and the ACLU Bill of Rights Award for her ongoing defense of constitutional rights; the recipient of the National Endowment for the Arts' National Medal of Arts

Family: married to director/actor James Brolin

Story: The resumé of Barbra Streisand is a map of success and celebrity: 43 gold albums, 27 platinum albums, 13 multi-platinum albums, 8 gold singles, 5 platinum singles, 5 gold videos, 2 platinum videos, 1 multi-platinum video. And that's just for her music. Her distinguished acting career includes 10 Emmys, 2 Academy Awards and 7 nominations, multiple Tonys and critics awards.

With 47 gold albums, she is second in the all-time charts, ahead of The Beatles and The Rolling Stones, exceeded only by Elvis. She is the only female artist ever to have achieved 13 multi-platinum albums. A recent poll by the Reuters news agency identified her as the favorite female singer of the 20th century.

A huge celebrity in films, *The Prince of Tides* was the first motion picture directed by its female star ever to receive a Best Director nomination from the Directors Guild of America, as well as seven Academy Award nominations. Barbra Streisand produced the heralded drama in addition to directing and starring in it. She won the New York Drama Critics Award and received a Tony nomination.

For her motion picture debut in *Funny Girl*, she won the 1968 Academy Award for Best Actress, the first of two Oscars. With *Yentl* in 1983, she became the first woman ever to produce, direct, write and star in a major motion picture.

www.barbrastreisand.com/statements.html#freepress

www.bjsmusic.com

The Essential Barbra Streisand

Her Name Is Barbra: An Intimate Portrait of the Real Barbra Streisand

59. Bob Proctor

Born in Ontario, Canada

Occupation: author, speaker

Claim to Fame: helps millions experience prosperity

Obstacles Faced: lack of education, poverty

Achievements: in one year went from destitute to an income over $100,000; now invites others to turn their lives around

Story: For four decades, Bob Proctor has focused his time, attention and energy on helping people create their own stories of success and achievement. He extends this invitation from a place of experience. Proctor knows what it's like to transform a life, because he comes from a background of want and limitation. In 1960, he was a high-school dropout with no job prospects and no hope. He happened upon Napoleon Hill's book *Think and Grow Rich*. In a very short time, with virtually no money or resources to his name, Proctor's life began to change. With further support from the works of Earl Nightingale, he was making more than $100,000 in a year and soon joined the ranks of self-made millionaires.

A real-life success story of the benefits of the resources of his real-life mentors, Earl Nightingale and Lloyd Conant, Proctor went to work for them. He worked his way up the ladder to the position of vice president of sales at Nightingale-Conant.

Later establishing his own seminar company, Proctor now travels the world teaching people how to believe in their own potential.

www.bobproctor.com
You Were Born Rich

60. Dr. Edward de Bono

Born in 1933 in Malta

Occupation: author, teacher, lecturer, held faculty positions at the universities of Oxford, Cambridge and Harvard; currently the chairman of the Council of Young Enterprise Europe

Claim to Fame: pioneer in the field of creative thinking

Obstacles Faced: when he began making breakthroughs, the field of creative thinking barely existed and was completely undervalued

Achievements: the founder of the Cognitive Research Trust and the International Creative Forum, which brings together many of the leading minds and think-tanks in the world; awarded numerous international awards; established the World Academy of New Thinking™, which is an association of those who believe in the need and importance for new thinking, new perceptions, fresh alternatives, a change of emphasis and the generation and design of new concepts and ideas; has a degree in medicine, an honors degree in psychology and physiology from Oxford; holds a Ph.D. from Cambridge

Family: married, with two sons

Story: Edward de Bono is regarded as one of the planet's leaders in the field of creative thinking. As an authority on thinking skills, he's written 62 books, which are translated into 37 languages.
The originator of the concept of lateral thinking, which treats creativity as the behavior of information in the brain, Dr. de Bono has developed formal tools and techniques of lateral, parallel and creative thinking. Many countries around the world use his methods and teachings as a mandatory part of the curriculum.

The appeal of Dr. de Bono's work is its simplicity and practicality. It can be used by children and by corporate executives, by Down Syndrome youngsters and Nobel laureates. In a nutshell, he teaches us how to think better.

www.en.wikipedia.org/wiki/Edward_De_Bono
www.edwdebono.com/index.html
New Thinking for the New Millennium
De Bono's Thinking Course

61. Jay Leno

Born in 1950 in New Rochelle, New York, USA

Occupation: host of NBC's *The Tonight Show*

Claim to Fame: *The Tonight Show* is the highest-rated late night talk show in the U.S.

Achievements: successor to the legendary Johnny Carson, numerous Emmy awards and a star on Hollywood's Walk of Fame

Family: married to Mavis Leno

Story: After earning a degree in speech therapy in Boston in 1973, Jay Leno went to pursue a profession as a stand-up comedian in Los Angeles. He actually made his *Tonight Show* debut in 1977, as a comedian guest. Starting in 1985, he filled in as guest host for Johnny Carson several times and in 1987 became the exclusive *Tonight Show* host.

When Johnny Carson announced his retirement, it was assumed that *The Tonight Show* torch would be passed on to David Letterman. But in an unexpected move, Leno was named Carson's successor, and he became the next to follow in the line of *Tonight Show* talents such as Steve Allen and Jack Paar.

Today, aside from his role as host, Leno continues to take his comedy act around the States, from Las Vegas to college campuses. He also travels overseas to entertain the troops working for the peace-keeping efforts in Bosnia.

Leno's children's book *If Roast Beef Could Fly* hit bookstores in April 2004 and immediately was a *New York Times* best seller.

The Tonight Show celebrated its 50th anniversary in September 2004. NBC announced that Jay Leno will remain at the helm until 2009, when he will be replaced by Conan O'Brien.

www.AskMen.com

www.nbc.com/The_Tonight_Show_with_Jay_Leno/bios/Jay_Leno.html

Leading with My Chin

Jay Leno's Headlines: Real but Ridiculous Headlines from America's Newspapers

62. Julia Cameron

Occupation: artist

Claim to Fame: advocates for the artist in all of us

Obstacles Faced: art and creativity is undervalued in our consumer society

Story: Julia Cameron is a popular and ground-breaking artist whose creativity refuses to be pigeonholed. Poet, novelist, filmmaker, playwright, producer and director, she is best known for her best-selling books, *The Artist's Way* and *The Right to Write.*

An advocate for the creative impulse that resides in all of us, Julia's greatest contribution is her passion for teaching others to tap into their innate creative source. She has debunked the myth that creativity is exclusive to artists. In Julia's world, we are all artists and are, therefore, obliged to discover the wellspring inside ourselves and express what we find there.

Once married to American movie director Martin Scorsese, she's collaborated with him on several films. Cameron has also taught film at such diverse places as Chicago Filmmakers, Northwestern University and Columbia College.

www.penguinputnam.com/static/packages/us/juliacameron/bio.html
The Artist's Way: a Spiritual Path to Higher Creativity
Walking in This World: The Practical Art of Creativity
The Vein of Gold

63. Katie Couric

Born in 1957 in Virginia, USA

Occupation: broadcast journalist

Claim to Fame: achieved celebrity status as host of *The Today Show* by touching the hearts of millions of Americans daily with her unique charm, warmth and accessibility

Obstacles Faced: husband Jay Monahan died in 1998 of colon cancer

Achievements: has worked for ABC news, CNN, NBC News, *Dateline, The Today Show;* maintains an astonishing balance of professional and personal life; named "Best in the Business" in 1993 by the *Washington Journalism Review;* won two Emmys and multiple other television journalism awards; named one of *Glamour* magazine's Women of the Year

Family: has two daughters

Story: Beloved by millions, Katie Couric is one of America's most recognizable and popular television news personalities. After just 11 years of marriage, her husband died of colon cancer. America watched her support him throughout his devastating illness. Then as she recovered from the shock of his death, she became outspoken for early testing of cancers. In 1999, Couric co-founded a non-profit organization for cancer research education.

She has been co-anchor of *The Today Show* since April 1991. With her perky attitude and inquisitive interviewing style, Couric boosted the show's sagging ratings, and she became of morning TV's most popular personalities. She's also a contributing anchor for *Dateline NBC.*

Rumors have it that the lively host could take over for *The NBC Nightly News* anchor Tom Brokaw when he retires in December 2004. Couric has filled in occasionally for Brokaw on the evening news program.

www.world-of-celebrities.com/katie_couric

www.geocities.com/couric_fan/bio.html

The Brand New Kid

Tales from the Bed: On Living, Dying, and Having It All

64. Laura Bush

Born in 1946 in Midland, Texas, USA

Occupation: first lady of the U.S.

Achievements: active in education, health and equal rights campaigns

Family: married to President Bush, with twin daughters

Story: With a unique career evolution, Laura Bush has been a school teacher, librarian and first lady of America.

Mrs. Bush earned a bachelor of science degree in education and a master of library science degree from the University of Texas. In 1977, she met and married George W. Bush. As first lady of Texas and now as first lady of the U.S., Laura Bush balances supporting her husband and raising her daughters with an active participation in initiatives in childhood education and literacy. As one of her first priorities as first lady, she convened the White House Summit on Early Childhood Cognitive Development.

The founder of a national initiative, Ready to Read, Ready to Learn, which educates the public about early childhood education and the importance of reading to children, she also developed a series of magazines called *Healthy Start, Grow Smart* to provide parents with information about their infant's cognitive development and health.

In collaboration with the Library of Congress, Mrs. Bush hosts the annual National Book Festival and the series "White House Salute to America's Authors," which celebrates great American literary works. Featured authors have included Mark Twain, Truman Capote, Flannery O'Connor and Eudora Welty.

A major advocate for women's equal rights, Laura Bush leads America's efforts to bring education to people worldwide, especially to women and girls. She's the only first lady in history to make a presidential radio address, where she spoke out on the plight of women and children living under the Afghanistan's Taliban regime.

A key player in education campaigns for breast cancer, heart disease and national preservation, she encourages Americans to get involved in preserving main streets, parks and community treasures.

www.whitehouse.gov/firstlady/flbio.html
The Perfect Wife: The Life and Choices of Laura Bush
George and Laura: Portrait of an American Marriage

65. Madeleine Albright

Born in 1937 in Prague, Czechoslovakia

Occupation: former U.S. ambassador to the United Nations; former U.S. secretary of state

Claim to Fame: America's first female secretary of state

Obstacles Faced: a political refugee as a child; as a woman (not to mention a foreign-born immigrant whose first language is not English), Albright has had to struggle against the tide of the 'old boy' establishment to achieve her goals

Achievements: earned a position of power in the American political arena, although English was not her first language

Family: divorced, with three daughters

Story: Madeleine Albright escaped her homeland with her family after a Communist coup in Czechoslovakia in 1948. The family was granted political asylum in the United States, where she became a naturalized U.S. citizen. She's fluent in English, Czech, French, Polish and Russian.

Following 20 years of working as a liaison to the National Security Council and as a professor of international affairs and the director of the Women in Foreign Service program at Georgetown University's School of Foreign Service, Albright was named U.S. ambassador to the United Nations by President Clinton in 1992.

She was, and is, dedicated to protecting cultural and ethnic diversity and religious freedom worldwide. This interest was heightened in 1997 when *The Washington Post* uncovered what Albright herself didn't know—that her heritage was Jewish, not Catholic, as she herself had believed up to that time. Her father had converted from Judaism to Catholicism in order to escape persecution.

www.abcnews.go.com/reference/bios/albright.html
www.nwhp.org/tlp/biographies/albright/albright_bio.html
Madam Secretary

66. Pelé

Born in 1940 in Brazil

Occupation: soccer champion

Claim to Fame: top soccer goal scorer of all-time

Obstacles Faced: poverty

Achievements: 1978 recipient of the International Peace Award; named athlete of the century in 1980 and 1999 by the National Olympics Committees

Story: Soccer, known as "The World's Game" is the most popular sport on the planet. There is no comparable phenomenon in North America—World Cup soccer wins or losses literally brings a country's commerce to a standstill as populations celebrate the joys of victories or the agonies of defeat in wild displays of emotion, patriotism and team loyalty. There is one name that every soccer fan knows and adores: Pelé.

Born Edson Arantes do Nascimento, he shined shoes for a meager living when he was discovered at age 11. He became a Brazilian national hero and was known as Perola Negra—Black Pearl. He led the Brazilian national soccer team to three World Cup victories in 1958, 1962 and 1970 and was the world's most famous and highest-paid athlete when he joined a North American team in 1975.

Over his career, from 1956 to 1977, he scored an unbelievable 1,281 goals in 1,363 games—an all-time world record the equivalent of a baseball player's hitting a home run in every World Series game for 15 consecutive years. No contemporary soccer superstar has ever scored 50 goals a season. Pelé scored 52 in the 1973 season.

He stopped a war—both sides in Nigeria's civil war called a 48-hour cease-fire in 1967 so Pelé could play an exhibition match in the capital of Lagos.

Pelé has also published best-selling autobiographies, starred in films and composed musical scores. He served as Brazil's minister of sport for a term.

www.360soccer.com/pele

www.time.com/time/time100/heroes/profile/pele01.html

www.ifhof.com/hof/pele.asp

My Life and the Beautiful Game: The Autobiography of Pelé

Pelé: His Life and Times

67. Dr. Stephen Hawking

Born in 1942 in Oxford, England

Occupation: physicist

Claim to Fame: one of the two greatest minds of our time

Obstacles Faced: lives with a motor neuron disease (ALS), a condition in which the nerves controlling the muscles die off, but the sensory nerves continue as before; it takes him 40 hours to prepare a 45-minute lecture

Achievements: advancing Einstein's theory of general relativity with quantum theory; has twelve honorary degrees, was awarded the CBE in 1982 and was made a Companion of Honor in 1989; the recipient of many awards, medals and prizes; is a Fellow of The Royal Society and a Member of the US National Academy of Sciences

Family: married, with three children and one grandchild

Story: Since 1979, Stephen Hawking has held the post of Lucasian Professor of Mathematics, a position once held by Sir Isaac Newton. Possibly the best-known scientist of our age, Hawking is an icon for the advances he brings to the world of quantum physics. And he makes it all accessible to the layperson with his best-selling books.

Diagnosed with ALS at age 21, he serves to inspire us all by overcoming his limitations in a way that seems impossible. An active lecturer and teacher, author and family man, he distances many of us who don't struggle with disabilities. Unable now to care for himself, to speak or to write, he uses an adaptive communication system called Equalizer, which includes a speech synthesizer. He's written a book, dozens of scientific papers and lectures internationally through the use of the Equalizer system. He's able to speak at a rate of 15 words a minute—far, far slower than the speed of his mind.

In 1988, he wrote the book *A Brief History of Time* that quickly leaped onto the best-seller list. It's been translated into 30 languages and has sold over 10 million copies worldwide. His two books, *A Brief History of Time* and *The Universe in a Nutshell*, have remained highly popular all over the world and remain classic best sellers.

www.en.wikipedia.org/wiki/Steven_Hawking

www.hawking.org.uk

A Brief History of Time

The Theory of Everything: The Origin and Fate of the Universe

68. Wayne Gretzky

Born in 1961 in Ontario, Canada

Occupation: hockey champion

Claim to Fame: greatest player in the history of hockey, a.k.a., The Great One

Obstacles Faced: disbelief

Achievements: in 1999, shortly after his retirement, Gretzky was inducted into the Hockey Hall of Fame; ESPN named Gretzky the fifth greatest athlete of the 20th century, voted #5 among North American athletes by *Sports Century;* following his final game, the NHL bestowed on Gretzky the unique distinction of being the only player in the history of the NHL to have his jersey number retired by all member clubs; "Number 99" was formally retired at the 2000 NHL All-Star Game in Toronto and will never again be worn by an NHL player; founder of the Wayne Gretzky Foundation, dedicated to helping disadvantaged youngsters throughout North America participate in hockey

Family: Gretzky and his wife Janet have five children

Story: A hockey prodigy by 16, Gretzky made headlines in 1979—his first season in the NHL with the Edmonton Oilers—when he won the trophy for the NHL's MVP. He was just 18 years old. He won MVP seven additional years running.

Early on in his career (1988), after helping Edmonton capture a fourth Stanley Cup, Gretzky was traded to the Los Angeles Kings in one of the biggest deals in sports history. Canada literally mourned the loss. Later traded to the New York Rangers, The Great One retired in 1999. At that time he held 61 NHL records.

In 1997, two years before he retired, The Hockey News put together a committee of 50 hockey experts, which included former NHL players, past and present writers, broadcasters, coaches and hockey executives.

He holds a total of nine MVP awards and is the only player in NHL history to record more than 200 points in a season. Gretzky is the most-honored player in any team sport.

www.upperdeck.com/athletes/waynegretzky/default.aspx
www.nhl.com/hockeyu/history/gretzky
The Great One: The Life and Times of Wayne Gretzky

69. Cheryl Richardson

Born in 1964 in Palo Alto, California, USA

Occupation: coach, author, speaker, television host, producer

Claim to Fame: one of the most sought-after motivational speakers in the country

Achievements: possibly the best-known life coach in America

Story: After a stint as a business counselor, Cheryl Richardson discovered a new field that was opening up that compelled her. Life coaching was basically unheard of when Richardson made the bold decision to leave her successful practice and study directly under the "father of coaching," Thomas Leonard. Earning her Master Coach certification in three years, Richardson exploded onto the self-development scene with seminars and programs that quickly gained popularity. Riding the first wave of life coaching, Richardson tapped into the public's desire for a balanced lifestyle, better relationships and motivation. It proved to be a winning formula.

Achieving instant recognition as a regular guest on *The Oprah Winfrey Show*, Richardson wrote several popular books and maintained a busy schedule of nationwide seminars and speeches. But the fame and the schedule took its toll. In 1997, Richardson faced a health crisis and chose to turn inward to regain a sense of balance and well-being. She learned to incorporate meditation into her daily life and soon recovered, with a strengthened sense of her spiritual core. She took her new-found wisdom public.

Famously rocking the boat by telling women that they needed to put themselves before their children, Richardson advocates self-care and balance to develop better parenting skills and relationships. Perhaps her greatest legacy will be the Lifestyle makeover groups, a free and leaderless system of people meeting and supporting each other.

www.cherylrichardson.com
Finding Your Passion
Take Time for Your Life

70. Archbishop Desmond Tutu

Born in 1931 in Klerksdorp, Transvaal

Occupation: Archbishop Emeritus of Cape Town, Professor of Theology at Emory University in Atlanta, human rights activist

Claim to Fame: fought apartheid and won

Obstacles Faced: a governmental regime of racism, oppression and violence

Achievements: general secretary of the South African Council; honorary doctor of a number of leading universities in the U.S., Britain and Germany; Nobel Peace Prize

Family: married to Leah Nomalizo Tutu, with four children

Story: In 1957, Desmond Tutu was a high school teacher in South Africa at the height of the government's Apartheid regime, the systematic program of racial segregation that existed in South Africa between 1948 and 1990. When a deliberately inferior educational system was legislated for black children, Tutu could no longer remain passive. He refused to cooperate with the state-sanctioned racism and stepped onto his life's true path.

Tutu began to study theology and was ordained as a priest in 1960. In 1975, he was appointed Dean of St. Mary's Cathedral in Johannesburg, the first black to hold that position. He later became the first black Anglican Archbishop of Cape Town, placing him at the head the Anglican Church in South Africa. Now he had the power and influence to take on apartheid.

It is for his pacifist opposition to apartheid that he earned 1984's Nobel Peace Prize. He worked tirelessly against the regime and gained the respect and cooperation of other world leaders. In 1990, Nelson Mandela, of the African National Congress, was released after almost 27 years in prison for opposing apartheid. After the country's first multi-racial elections in 1994, President Mandela appointed Archbishop Tutu to chair the Truth and Reconciliation Commission, investigating the human rights violations of the previous 34 years. As always, the Archbishop counseled forgiveness and cooperation, rather than revenge for past injustice.

www.nobelprize.org/peace/laureates/1984/tutu-bio.html

www.tutu.org

God Has a Dream : A Vision of Hope for Our Time

No Future Without Forgiveness

71. Dr. Jane Goodall

Born in 1934 in London, England

Occupation: primatologist

Claim to Fame: legendary for her work in her field, Dr. Goodall has brought a once-obscure study to the attention of the mainstream

Obstacles Faced: has a neurological condition known as prosopagnosia, which is a memory impairment for face and patterns; husband died of cancer; at the time she began her studies and field work, it was unheard of for a woman to do so

Achievements: gave legitimacy to women scientists, conservatism and a new way to understand animals; in 2003, Queen Elizabeth II named Dr. Goodall a Dame of the British Empire, the equivalent of knighthood; received honorary doctorates from numerous universities; other honors include the Medal of Tanzania, the National Geographic Society's Hubbard Medal, Japan's prestigious Kyoto Prize, the Prince of Asturias Award for Technical and Scientific Research, the Benjamin Franklin Medal in Life Science and the Gandhi/King Award for Nonviolence; in April 2002, Secretary-General Annan named Dr. Goodall a United Nations "Messenger of Peace"

Story: In 1960, 26-year-old Jane Goodall went to Lake Tanganyika in East Africa to study the area's chimpanzee population. She defied scientific convention by practically joining groups of primates and by studying them non-invasively.

Her observations and discoveries are internationally recognized as the best in the field. Her research into the biology and sociology of chimpanzees is making revolutionary inroads into scientific thinking regarding the evolutions of our own species.

Today the Jane Goodall Institute for Wildlife Research, Education and Conservation empowers people to make a difference for all living things and provides ongoing support for field research on wild chimpanzees. For more than three decades, Goodall's work has set new standards in all the sciences and opened new doors in our understanding of our place in the animal kingdom.

www.janegoodall.org
www.pbs.org/wnet/nature/goodall
www.nationalgeographic.com/council/eir/bio_goodall.html
Jane Goodall: 40 Years at Gombe
In the Shadow of Man

72. Jay Abraham

Occupation: business guru, marketing consultant

Claim to Fame: America's highest-paid marketing consultant

Obstacles Faced: changing marketing trends, recessions, the transition to a global economy

Achievements: as the founder and CEO of Abraham Group, Inc. in Los Angeles, California, Abraham has spent the last 25 years creating windfall profits for his clients; the March 6, 2000 issue of *Forbes Magazine* listed him as one of the top five executive coaches in the country

Story: Worldwide, there are about 10,000 business owners in 400 industries who go to bed happy at night and laugh all the way to the bank thanks to help from one man. Jay Abraham has achieved almost legendary status across the business landscape for increasing business income, wealth and success.

He's been said to possess an uncanny ability to think "way outside the box" and to produce the results lauded by entrepreneurs: lower risks, solved problems, higher revenues and multiplied assets. Many businesses credit Abraham's efforts and ideas with a profit increase in the millions of dollars. He's been featured twice in *Investors Business Daily*. In addition, he's been written up in *USA Today, The New York Times, The Los Angeles Times, The Washington Post, The San Francisco Chronicle, OTC Stock Journal, National Underwriter, Entrepreneur, Success* and *Inc.* magazines and many others.

A unique authority on business strategy, innovation, marketing and management, Abraham quickly finds overlooked opportunities, hidden assets and underperforming areas of a business that others miss.

Having made literally billions of dollars for others, he's become both a millionaire and a guru of business success. A generation of marketing experts credits him as their primary mentor.

www.abraham.com/index.html

Getting Everything You Can Out of All You've Got:
21 Ways You Can Out-Think, Out-Perform, and Out-Earn the
Competition

73. John Grisham

Born in 1955 in Arkansas, USA

Occupation: best-selling author, former member of Congress

Claim to Fame: the master of the legal thriller

Obstacles Faced: dislikes publicity and fame

Achievements: since first publishing *A Time to Kill* in 1988, every book he's written has become a best seller; *Publishers Weekly* named him "the best-selling novelist of the 90s"

Family: wife Renee, with two children

Story: Grisham earned a law degree in 1981 at the University of Mississippi. He established a law practice in Southaven, where he practiced both criminal and civil law. In 1983, he was elected to the Mississippi House of Representatives. In 1989, he published his first novel *A Time to Kill*, which has since been made into a Hollywood film. His next book, *The Firm*, was his break-out hit. Even before the book was published, Paramount Pictures purchased the film rights.

In 1990, he resigned from the House of Representatives and bought a farm near Oxford, Mississippi. With 17 fictions and 7 films under his belt, Grisham is distinguished with the reputation as the master of the legal thriller. In fact, it was during his stellar career as author that he bagged his biggest legal verdict ever, for a special case he fought in 1996. He returned to the courtroom after a five-year hiatus in order to honor a commitment made before he had retired from the law to become a full-time writer. He represented the family of a railroad brakeman killed when he was pinned between two cars. Approaching the case with the passion he approaches his writing, Grisham successfully argued his client's case, earning them a jury award of $683,500.

When he's not writing, Grisham devotes time to charitable causes, including the creation of six baseball fields he built on his property, which have played host to over 350 kids on 26 Little League teams. He also serves as the local Little League commissioner.

www.randomhouse.com/features/grisham
www.en.wikipedia.org/wiki/John_Grisham
The Last Juror
The Firm
The Pelican Brief

74. Mikhail Gorbachev

Born in 1931 in Privolnoye, Russia

Occupation: chairperson of the Gorbachev Foundation and consultant to world leaders

Claim to Fame: former president of the Soviet Union

Obstacles Faced: the collapse of communism, the end of the Soviet Union

Achievements: key player in ending the Cold War; opened the door to democracy in Eastern Europe; awarded the Nobel peace prize in 1990

Story: Mikhail Gorbachev, at age 54, was elected general secretary of the Communist Party in March 1985, after the death of Konstantin Chernenko. As the de facto ruler of the Soviet Union, his priority was to reform the declining Communist Party rule, as well as resuscitate the state economy. To this end, he famously introduced the principles and policies of glasnost (openness) and perestroika (restructuring).

In 1988, Gorbachev announced that the Soviet Union would abandon the stagnant Brezhnev Doctrine and allow the Eastern European countries to democratize, if they wished. This led to the series of revolutions in eastern Europe, in which Communism collapsed. With the exception of Romania, the collapses were all peaceful ones.

These events ended the Cold War, but the democratization of the USSR and Eastern Europe tore away the power of the Communist party and himself, and conservatives in the Soviet leadership launched the August Coup in 1991 in an attempt to remove Gorbachev from power. To the amazement of people all over the world, the once-powerful Soviet Union disintegrated by December 1991. Gorbachev resigned as President on Christmas Day.

In 1992, he became the head of The Foundation for Social, Economic and Political Research, an international think tank. Today Gorbachev heads the Gorbachev Foundation, which provides in-depth analysis of the evolving social, economic and political situation in Russia and in the world.

www.mikhailgorbachev.org

Conversations with Gorbachev

The Gorbachev Phenomenon: A Historical Interpretation

75. Peter Jackson

Born in 1961 in Pukerua Bay, New Zealand

Occupation: movie director, writer, producer

Claim to Fame: directed and adapted J.R.R. Tolkien's epic fantasy trilogy *The Lord of the Rings*

Obstacles Faced: obscurity

Achievements: National Board of Review: Special Achievement Award, *The Lord of the Rings: The Fellowship of the Ring* (2001); BAFTA: Best Film, *The Lord of the Rings: The Fellowship of the Ring* (2002); Oscar: Best Director, *The Lord of the Rings: The Return of the King* (2004); Oscar: Best Picture, *The Lord of the Rings: The Return of the King* (2004); Oscar: Adapted Screenplay, *The Lord of the Rings: The Return of the King* (2004)

Family: married to Frances Walsh since 1987, with two children

Story: Jackson started filmmaking at age twelve with an 8mm camera. First known for his slapstick horror comedies, he became somewhat known for his movie *Heavenly Creatures*, for which he shared an Oscar nomination for Best Screenplay Written Directly for the Screen with Fran Walsh.

Jackson is now world renowned as the director of the epic film trilogy *The Lord of the Rings*, based on the books by J. R. R. Tolkien. As of 2004, the trilogy made him the highest-paid motion picture director in history. He won three Academy Awards for *The Lord of the Rings: The Return of the King*, the third film of the trilogy.

Currently in the works is a remake of the 1933 classic *King Kong*. The film will be released during the Christmas season of 2005.

www.eonline.com/Facts/People/Bio/0,128,7728,00.html?celfact1
www.en.wikipedia.org/wiki/Peter_Jackson
www.lordoftherings.net/film/filmmakers/fi_pjack.html
Peter Jackson: From Gore to Mordor

76. Robin Williams

Born in 1952 in Chicago, Illinois, USA

Occupation: comedian, actor

Claim to Fame: earned respect and accolades as a serious actor

Obstacles Faced: substance abuse, depression

Achievements: 30 awards over 25 years, including 1989's American Comedy Award for Funniest Stand-Up Comedian

Family: married, with three children

Story: Robin Williams was an audience favorite on the comedy circuit in the 1970's. But Williams' career blasted off in 1978 when he was cast as Mork from Ork, the alien on the hit sitcom *Mork and Mindy*. The show ran for four seasons and earned Williams a Golden Globe Award for Best Actor in a Television Series.

During the 1980's, Williams' star started its slow rise in feature films, such as *Popeye*, *The World According to Garp* and 1984's *Moscow on the Hudson*. In 1987, he achieved superstardom with his role in *Good Morning, Vietnam.*

The 90's proved to be a better decade for Williams. He earned two Oscar nominations for his work in *Dead Poet's Society* and *Awakenings*. In 1991, *The Fisher King* earned him the Best Actor Golden Globe and another Oscar nomination. He went drag in *Mrs. Doubtfire* a year later, a film that made over $200 million in the U.S. alone and earning Williams a Golden Globe Award, People's Choice Award and an MTV Movie Award. *Good Will Hunting* came next and then *Insomnia*, both of which were relatively dark roles for Williams. He decisively proved his ability to play dark roles in 2002 with the creepy *One Hour Photo*.

Robin Williams and his wife Marsha Garces Williams founded the Windfall Foundation, a philanthropic organization to raise money for many different charities. Robin Williams generously works for charities, including the Comic Relief fund-raising efforts.

www.askmen.com/men/entertainment_60/96c_robin_williams.html
www.robin-williams.net
www.en.wikipedia.org/wiki/Robin_Williams
Robin Williams
The Life and Humor of Robin Williams: A Biography

77. Sir Sean Connery

Born in 1930 in Edinburgh, Scotland

Occupation: actor, philanthropist

Claim to Fame: widely considered THE James Bond

Obstacles Faced: lack of education

Achievements: renowned as one of the best actors of the era, knighted by Queen Elizabeth II on New Year's Eve in 1999, received the Freedom of the City of Edinburgh in 1991, awarded multiple awards for his performances

Family: married to his second wife (of more than 25 years), with one son with his first wife

Story: A child of the Great Depression, Thomas Sean Connery always had the drive to earn money—whether it was by delivering milk or polishing coffins. A 13-year-old Connery left school and soon joined the Royal Navy at 15.

After his stint in the Navy, Connery held a variety of odd jobs, most notably posing for art classes and swimsuit ads. Modeling led to an interest in bodybuilding, and at 20, he made third place in the Mr. Universe competition. Of course, his career was defined when he was cast as the suave secret agent 007 in the first of the James Bond films, 1962's *Dr. No.* Several other actors took a turn in the role of Bond, but Connery is considered *the* James Bond.

Heartthrob, action-star and consummate hero, Sir Sean's acting career spans 40 years and countless award-winning performances. Famously donating tens of thousands of dollars to help flood victims in Prague in 2003, he also donates time and money to a United Nations food agency: the World Food Program.

One of the most acclaimed actors of our age, his personal appeal has not faded with age. In 1989, at almost 60 years of age, he was voted *People* magazine's "Sexiest Man Alive." When advised of the award, Sean shrugged it off replying, "Well there aren't many sexy dead men, are there."

www.askmen.com
www.seanconnery.com
Sean Connery: A Biography
The Films of Sean Connery

78. Susan Sarandon

Born in 1946 in New York City, USA

Occupation: actor, activist

Claim to Fame: appeared in over 50 films over 34 years

Achievements: Genie Awards for Best Actress; named Actress of the Year in 1991 by the London Film Critics Circle; Screen Actors Guild Awards; Oscar for Best Actress, *Dead Man Walking*

Family: three children—two with long-time companion, actor Tim Robbins

Story: First rising out of relative obscurity in 1975 with her lead role in cult classic *The Rocky Horror Picture Show*, Susan Sarandon also played the female lead in *The Great Waldo Pepper* that year opposite Robert Redford.

Although nominated for an Oscar in 1980 for *Atlantic City*, she did not become a household name until 1988's *Bull Durham*. It was the following decade—the 1990's—that brought Sarandon her biggest accolades with four Academy Award nominations, including one for *Thelma & Louise*. She finally won the Oscar in 1996 for her role in *Dead Man Walking* with Sean Penn.

Sarandon and her mate Robbins are known also for their activism in numerous political, cultural and health causes.

www.biography.com/search/article.jsp?aid=9471729&search
www.search.eb.com/women/articles/Sarandon_Susan.html
Susan Sarandon: A True Maverick
Susan Sarandon: Actress-Activist

79. Suze Orman

Born in 1961 in Chicago, Illinois, USA

Occupation: author, speaker, certified financial planner

Claim to Fame: financial guru to millions

Obstacles to Overcome: diagnosed with a speech impediment in early childhood, it severely affected her ability to learn how to read

Achievements: the author of the *New York Times* best-sellers *The 9 Steps to Financial Freedom* and *The Courage to Be Rich;* recognized by *Smart Money* magazine as one of its top thirty "Power Brokers"

Family: lives with her family in California

Story: Suze Orman launched her own financial planning and consulting firm in 1987 after a successful stint working for big firms such as Merrill Lynch and Prudential. With her own company, Orman was able to develop her unique brand of financial counseling —one that would immediately catch on as practical and popular.

She literally transformed the concept of personal finance by teaching us about our relationship with money and how to nurture it. Orman digs deeper than the run-of-the-mill money management tips and offers us awareness of the psychological—even spiritual power— money has in our lives.

Orman has hosted two PBS specials based on her books and has appeared numerous times on *Oprah, Good Morning America,* CNN and several other major television programs. She is a financial contributor to NBC News and appears regularly on QVC as host of her own "Financial Freedom" hour.

Her best-selling books, *The 9 Steps to Financial Freedom* and *The Courage to Be Rich,* are considered "must reads" for anyone with a desire to reach their financial goals.

www.suzeorman.com/home.asp

The 9 Steps to Financial Freedom

The Courage to Be Rich: Creating a Life of Material and Spiritual Abundance

The Road to Wealth: A Comprehensive Guide to Your Money : Everything You Need to Know in Good and Bad Times

80. Ted Turner

Born in 1938 in Cincinnati, Ohio, USA

Occupation: media mogul, philanthropist

Claim to Fame: founded CNN and headed up one of the largest media companies in the world

Obstacles Faced: his father's suicide

Achievements: holds numerous honorary degrees, industry awards and civic honors, including being named *Time* magazine's 1991 Man of the Year and Cable and Broadcasting's Man of the Century in 1999; inducted into the Cable TV Hall of Fame in 1999; in June 2000 he received the World Ecology Award from the University of Missouri; a world-class yachtsman, he earned national and world sailing titles and four Yachtsman of the Year awards

Family: divorced from actor Jane Fonda, with five children

Story: A billionaire many times over, Ted Turner represents true American wealth. His wealth manifested because he saw something that needed changing—the media—and made it happen.

As one of the planet's richest individuals, Turner owns the Atlanta Braves baseball club because he loves baseball. He inaugurated the Cable News Network (CNN), the world's first, live, in-depth, round-the-clock news television network because he believed the media could do better. He pioneered the notion of TV "super-station" broadcasting to cable systems nationwide by means of satellite because the technology existed. The system, later dubbed TBS (Turner Broadcasting Station), enters almost 200 million homes in approximately 200 countries and in nearly 40 languages. He bought Time Warner and Metro-Goldwyn-Mayer (MGM)/United Artists to round off his media empire.

Turner believes the more you earn, the more you should give. He founded the Turner Foundation to support environmental causes and donated $1 billion to the United Nations. He also launched the Goodwill Games in 1985 as an international, world-class, quadrennial, multi-sport competition.

www.turner.com/

www.turnerfoundation.org

Ted Turner: It Ain't As Easy as It Looks: A Biography

Me and Ted Against the World:
The Unauthorized Story of the Founding of CNN

81. Tom Brokaw

Born in 1940 in South Dakota, USA

Occupation: anchor person, managing editor of NBC Nightly News

Claim to Fame: the face of NBC News

Achievements: holds many journalistic firsts; has earned virtually every journalistic award out there, as well as seven Emmys for ground-breaking reports of significant world issues

Family: married, with three daughters

Story: At 6pm weekdays, more North Americans turn to Tom Brokaw than any other evening news anchor person. As the face of the highest-rated television evening news show—NBC News—for the past 20 years, Brokaw conveys a famously optimistic and easygoing delivery of the news we trust.

Besides being the most-trusted anchor person, he's also Managing Editor of *NBC Nightly News*. For the last 30 years, Tom Brokaw has had a big role in reporting the world's events.

He was the first person from the U.S. to have a one-on-one interview with Mikhail Gorbachev, the first anchor to report live from the Berlin Wall when it fell, to report the human rights abuses in Tibet and to interview the Dalai Lama. He was NBC's White House correspondent from 1973 to 1976 and has covered every presidential election since 1968. Brokaw will step down as anchor in December 2004.

A best-selling author, his books, *The Greatest Generation* and *The Greatest Generation Speaks*, are dedicated to Americans who experienced the Great Depression and World War II. He's written for several leading publications, including *The New York Times, The Washington Post, The Los Angeles Times, Newsweek, Sports Illustrated, Life* and *Interview*.

Brokaw regularly volunteers for Habitats and donated $250,000 toward a hiking and biking trail in his former hometown Yankton, South Dakota.

www.en.wikipedia.org/wiki/Tom_Brokaw

www.msnbc.msn.com/id/3032619

The Greatest Generation

A Long Way Home: Growing Up in the American Heartland in the Forties and Fifties

82. Tom Cruise

Born in 1962 in Syracuse, New York, USA

Occupation: actor

Claim to Fame: superstar actor

Obstacles Faced: diagnosed with dyslexia at age seven, he struggled to read and write

Achievements: one of Hollywood's most bankable names, multiple artistic awards, as well as awards for his charitable contributions to education and literacy

Family: divorced from actor Nicole Kidman, with two children

Story: Ask almost anyone to name an A-list male movie star, and they'll likely say Tom Cruise. The name alone conjures up an image of the megawatt smile of an actor who has earned his place in the rarefied air of superstardom.

Cruise navigated the rocky road from obscurity to celebrity with a grace that made us want to root for him. From the confident, smart, dynamic youth in the films of the 1980s, to the confident, smart, dynamic man of his most recent films, Cruise's star shot to stardom through the 80s and 90s and shows no sign of slowing. Cruise is an icon of superstardom. His flashing smile represents that ultimate combination of talent, fortune, luxury, access and star-mystique.

Cruise is a founding board member of the Hollywood Education and Literacy Project, a non-profit group that develops literacy in five countries.

www.askmen.com
www.helplearn.org
Tom Cruise: Unauthorized
Tom Cruise: A Biography

83. Walter Cronkite

Born in 1916 in St. Joseph, Missouri, USA

Occupation: retired journalist

Claim to Fame: most-famous TV anchorman

Achievements: named "the most trusted man in America" in a nationwide opinion poll in 1995, more than 10 years after leaving CBS as anchor; only journalist to be voted among the top ten "most influential decision makers in America" in surveys conducted by *U.S. News*. Named the "most influential person" in broadcasting; earned many journalism awards and honorary degrees and Emmys; awarded the Presidential Medal of Freedom in 1981

Story: Walter Cronkite joined the United Press in 1937 and worked there for 11 years, covering major world events, including major World War II battles and the Nuremberg trials for head Nazis, such as, Hermann Goering and Rudolf Hess. He also served as chief correspondent for the United Press in Moscow.

Best known for his work as the face of the evening news, Cronkite served as anchorman of the *CBS Evening News* from 1962 until 1981. In the collective consciousness of North Americans, his image and voice are closely associated with such watershed events as the Cuban missile crisis, the assassination of President John F. Kennedy, the Vietnam War, the Apollo 11 moon landing and the Watergate scandal. His signature sign-off, " . . . and that's the way it is" still echoes in our minds.

The Walter Cronkite School of Journalism & Mass Communication is part of Arizona State University.

www.cronkite.asu.edu

www.en.wikipedia.org/wiki/Walter_Cronkite

A Reporter's Life

Cronkite Remembers

84. Andre Agassi

Born in 1970 in Las Vegas, Nevada, USA

Occupation: tennis champion

Claim to Fame: highest-ranked tennis player in the world, over almost 20 years

Obstacles Faced: stunning comeback after being ranked 141st in 1997

Achievements: won four Grand Slams (the Grand Slams are the four most prestigious competitions in tennis) and won virtually every tennis award that exists

Family: married to fellow tennis champion Steffi Graf, with one child

Story: Andre Agassi was a tennis prodigy at age three. He turned pro in 1986 at the age of 16. A mere 24 months later, the youth was ranked 4th in the world. Rocking the then-staid and rarefied world of elite tennis, Andre took it by storm with his long hair and wild outfits. Appealing to a broader audience than ever before, tennis never looked the same and the world never looked back.

In 1994, he won the US Open, and that's when things really started to roll. In 1995, he achieved the top-ranked position in the world. In 1996, he won an Olympic gold medal. In 1999 (after marrying and divorcing celebrity Brooke Shields), Agassi became only the 5th player in history to win all four Grand Slams. With innumerable titles since, there isn't much that Agassi hasn't accomplished in the tennis world.

Famously in 1992, on winning his first Grand Slam title, he fell to his knees and cried. He has since earned the title an additional six times.

With a strong desire to make a further contribution to the world, he founded the Andre Agassi Charitable Association, which assists youth. In 1995, he won the ATP Arthur Ashe's Humanitarian award in recognition of his efforts helping disadvantaged youth in Los Angeles.

www.agassifoundation.org

www.usopen.org/en_US/bios/ms/atpa092.html

www.askmen.com/men/sports/39_andre_agassi.html

Agassi and Ecstasy: The Turbulent Life of Andre Agassi

85. Barbara Bush

Born in 1925 in New York, USA

Occupation: former first lady of America, chairperson of The Barbara Bush Foundation

Claim to Fame: matriarch of the Bush family

Obstacles Faced: death of her daughter from leukemia

Achievements: advancing children's literacy

Family: married to President George Bush, Sr., with six children

Story: Toward the end of World War II, Barbara Bush met the man who would become her husband and the 41st president. They were married in 1945.

Today Mrs. Bush is the respected matriarch of the Bush family. Enjoying achievements such as a husband and a son becoming the leader of the free world, the family has also experienced tragedy. The Bush's daughter Robin died of leukemia at three years of age. Naturally devastated by the loss, the family eventually found a new strength from the experience. She says, "because of Robin, George and I love every living human more."

When her husband was vice president to Ronald Reagan, Mrs. Bush first became active in the promotion of literacy. It became her special cause. As first lady, she called working for a more literate America the "most important issue we have" and was honorary chairman of the Barbara Bush Foundation for Family Literacy. An advocate of volunteerism, Mrs. Bush also devoted her energy to causes, such as, the homeless, AIDS, the elderly and school volunteer programs.

www.womensissues.about.com/library/bio/blbio_bush_barbara.htm

www.whitehouse.gov/history/firstladies/bb41.html

Barbara Bush: a Memoir

Reflections: Life After the White House

86. Celine Dion

Born in 1968 in Quebec, Canada

Occupation: singer, songwriter

Claim to Fame: one of the biggest stars in pop music history, selling more than 100 million albums worldwide

Obstacles Faced: humble beginnings as 1 of 14 children; English is her second language, husband's throat cancer, a struggle with infertility

Achievements: Academy awards, Grammy awards, People's Choice award

Family: married, with one son

Story: When the 12-year-old Celine sang for a music executive in his office, he cried and then set in motion the process of making her a star. This man, Rene Angelil, later became her husband in 1994 in Montreal's Notre Dame Basilica. Their wedding was celebrated not only by the 250 invited guests but by millions of fans worldwide.

In the early 1990's, the theme song of Disney's *Beauty and the Beast* was her major international breakthrough. The song reached number one on the pop charts and won both a Grammy and an Academy award. Celine's other huge hit, the theme song for the blockbuster movie Titanic, *My Heart Will Go On*, became popular all over the world.

In 2002, Dion announced a three-year, 600-show contract to appear five nights a week in an entertainment extravaganza called *A New Day* at Caesar's Palace, Las Vegas. The production takes place in a custom-built, 4,000-seat theatre.

www.vh1.com/artists/az/dion_celine/bio.jhtml
www.celinedion.com/
Celine: The Authorized Biography
Celine Dion: My Story, My Dream

87. David Letterman

Born in 1947 in Indianapolis, Indiana, USA

Occupation: host of CBS's *Late Night with David Letterman*

Claim to Fame: one of *TV Guide*'s "50 Greatest TV Stars of All Time", 2000

Obstacles Faced: quintuple heart bypass surgery

Achievements: *The New York Observer* called Letterman "the gold standard for TV in our age" while *The New York Daily News* called him "the best the medium can achieve," 13 Emmys and 74 Emmy nominations

Family: became a father in 2003 at age 56

Story: A radio and television graduate of Ball State University, Letterman was a radio talk show host, a children's program host and a television weatherman before hitting his stride as guest host on *The Tonight Show* with Johnny Carson. After guest hosting 50 times, Letterman was given his own late-night show by NBC. *Late Night with David Letterman* debuted on February 1, 1982 and very rapidly garnered a cult-like following and critical acclaim.

Letterman's relationship with NBC soured when Johnny Carson retired and NBC reneged on their promise to have David Letterman take over his spot. Letterman moved to CBS and developed a late-night rivalry with Jay Leno, who succeeded Johnny Carson.

Next to Johnny Carson, he has the second longest run on late night TV. He brings $120 million in advertising to CBS a year.

Letterman was the first of the late-night talk show hosts to return to the air after the tragedies of 9/11. He deviated that evening from his usual opening monologue and sang "America the Beautiful" with Dan Rather and Regis Philbin.

www.AskMen.com

www.cbs.com/latenight/lateshow/show_info
  bios/ls_show_info_bios_dletterman.shtml

David Letterman's Book of Top Ten Lists

The Sweetheart of Sigma Chi: David Letterman, the College Years

88. Gloria Steinem

Born in 1934 in Ohio, USA

Occupation: writer, editor, activist

Claim to Fame: one of the most important voices of the modern feminist movement

Obstacles Faced: her mother suffered from a debilitating mental illness; did not attend school regularly until age 10; when her father abandoned the family, she was forced to run the household at age 11

Achievements: perhaps best known as the co-founder of *Ms.* magazine; named Woman of the Year in 1972 by *McCall's* magazine; inducted into the Women's Hall of Fame in 1993; inducted into the American Society of Magazine Editors Hall of Fame in 1998

Family: married in 2000, widowed in 2003

Story: After working as a television writer (an unusual position for a woman at the time) and working for Senator George McGovern's presidential campaign, Gloria Steinem landed a good position at *New York* magazine. There her writing created a national stir, and she garnered respect for her views on women's equality.

In 1971, she co-founded the first mass circulation feminist magazine *Ms.* The preview issue sold out and within five years had a circulation of 500,000. As editor of the magazine, Steinem gained national attention as a feminist leader and became an influential spokesperson for women's rights issues.

Gloria Steinem established the Ms. Foundation for Women, devoted to helping the lives of women and girls in three main categories: economic security, leadership and health and safety. She was a convener of the historic 1971 Women's Political Caucus, supported the founding of the Coalition of Labor Union Women and is president of Voters for Choice.

Her 1992 book, *Revolution from Within: A Book of Self-Esteem*, was a number-one best seller and has been translated into 11 languages.

www.motherjones.com/news/qa/1995/11/gorney.html
www.theglassceiling.com/biographies/bio32.htm
www.galegroup.com/free_resources/whm/bio/steinem_g.htm
Outrageous Acts and Everyday Rebellions
Revolution from Within: A Book of Self-Esteem

89. John Travolta

Born in 1954 in New Jersey, USA

Occupation: actor, pilot

Claim to Fame: ranked #21 in *Empire* magazine's "top 100 movie stars of all time"

Achievements: successfully balancing superstardom with a strong family life; numerous Golden Globe Awards, critic's awards and MTV Awards, named "Star of the Year" by NATO in 1983 and 1996

Family: married to actor Kelly Preston, with two children

Story: By the age of 12, John Travolta was performing in musicals and theater productions. He believed so fervently in his calling that he dropped out of high school at the age of 16 to pursue his acting career full time. He made his way to the Big Apple and started to get some work in a few Off-Broadway productions. His big break came in 1975, when the bright-eyed and boyish John was cast on the sitcom *Welcome Back Kotter* as Vinnie Barbarino.

Travolta was an overnight superstar and teen-idol. He made a smooth transition onto the silver screen and danced his way to mega-movie stardom in 1977's *Saturday Night Fever.* The film became the signature for the disco generation, and he earned an Oscar nomination for his now-iconic role.

In 1978, Travolta starred opposite Olivia Newton-John in *Grease.* It was an even greater hit than *Saturday Night Fever.* Travolta's fame was considered at its peak, especially when his career flagged slightly during the 1980's. But Travolta was restored to Hollywood's A-list with 1994's *Pulp Fiction.* Ever since, his ability to draw audiences and to impress them has been evident in a string of successful movies, most recently *Ladder 49,* Hollywood's ode to firefighters.

Travolta has appeared in 41 movies since 1975. He's a qualified pilot and owns five planes. One of his several homes has its own runway and taxiway right to the front door.

He's also an active member of the Church of Scientology.

www.travolta.com/news.htm

www.en.wikipedia.org/wiki/John_Travolta

John Travolta: Back in Character

Propeller One-Way Night Coach: A Story

90. Julia Roberts

Born in 1967 in Georgia, USA

Occupation: actor

Claim to Fame: tied with actor Cameron Diaz for the position of Hollywood's top female earner in the 2003 Hollywood Reporter Women In Entertainment list

Obstacles Faced: her father died of cancer when she was ten years old

Achievements: one of the most powerful celebrities, according to 2003 *Forbes* Top 100 Celebrity List (#21); Oscar, Golden Globe and People's Choice awards

Family: married to cameraman Danny Moder, with twins

Story: Julia Roberts' screen debut was only a decade and a half ago. Since that time, she's been one of the biggest and brightest of the Hollywood stars. An unknown in *Mystic Pizza*, her charm and sparkle were immediately evident and she landed a plum role in *Steel Magnolia*, with movie heavy-hitters Sally Field, Shirley MacLaine and Dolly Parton. Her portrayal earned her an Oscar nomination.

In a leap from respected actress to international superstar, Roberts played the role of a likeable prostitute in 1990's *Pretty Woman*. The film was a hit, and she was well on her way to being the most bankable woman in Hollywood.

Roberts once again earned recognition as a respected actress when she won an Oscar for her part as the title role in *Erin Brockovich* in 2000. With this movie, she proved once and for all that her enormous popularity was more than a pretty face and dazzling smile.

Her personal life finally matched the fairy tale status of her professional life when she found and married her soul mate, cameraman Danny Moder. The couple married in a midnight ceremony on Independence Day, July 4, 2002 at Roberts' ranch in New Mexico. She gave birth to twins (a boy and a girl) on November 28, 2004.

www.juliarobertsonline.com
www.aboutjulia.com
www.web.pinknet.cz/JuliaRoberts
www.entertainment.msn.com/celebs/celeb.aspx?mp=b&c=167068
Julia: Her Life
Julia Roberts: Confidential

91. Lee Iacocca

Born in 1924 in Allentown, Pennsylvania, USA

Occupation: industrialist

Claim to Fame: fathered present-day structure of the auto industry

Obstacles Faced: old-world business beliefs

Achievements: introduced leading-edge ideas to the auto industry; founder of The Lee Iacocca Diabetes Foundation; Iacocca has been a long-time supporter of diabetes and treatment since his wife Mary died from complications of the disease in 1983

Story: Starting as a fledgling sales person for Ford, Lee Iacocca climbed his way up the ranks with his innovative ideas. He was responsible for many unique ideas during the 1950s, including financing, which made the expensive cars accessible to the average family. As senior executive at Ford, he was responsible for the design of the Ford Mustang, Mercury Cougar and Lincoln Mark III.

Eventually Iacocca became the President of the Ford Motor Division but was forced to leave in 1978 because of a conflict with Henry Ford. He was snapped up by the Chrysler Corporation, which was on the verge of bankruptcy. Iacocca took the position and rebuilt the entire company from the ground up. In an unprecedented and controversial move, he went before the U.S. Congress in 1979 and asked for money. He pointed to the government bail-outs of the airline and railroad industry and argued that more jobs would be lost without the injection of capital. He got the money from the government and eventually repaid the entire loan.

Under Iacocca's direction, Chrysler released the K-car in 1980—a small, inexpensive automobile that sold rapidly after the 1970's oil crisis. In addition, Chrysler released the first minivan, and to this day, Chrysler leads sales of the minivan. Iacocca left Chrysler in 1992. He currently works with a company making electric bicycles.

Currently, Iacocca is the founder and chairman of the Advisory Board of the Iacocca Institute. Its goal is to make American industry more competitive in the international marketplace. He's also the chairman of the Iacocca Foundation, dedicated to educational projects and the advancement of diabetes research.

www.en.wikipedia.org/wiki/Lee_Iacocca

Iacocca: An Autobiography

Behind The Wheel At Chrysler: The Iacocca Legacy

92. Maria Shriver

Born in 1955 in Chicago, Illinois, USA

Occupation: journalist, author, first lady of California

Achievements: balancing marriage, motherhood, celebrity, charitable work and politics, while maintaining an active, award-winning career; multiple journalistic awards and accolades

Family: married, with four children

Story: Maria Shriver comes from a famous family, married a famous man, and her career revolved around interviewing famous people. Yet no one has ever doubted her own talents, charisma and intelligence. This is not a woman propped up by where she comes from or whom she knows. Shriver is a powerhouse in her own right.

A respected veteran TV news reporter and the niece of former American president John F. Kennedy, she married action movie star Arnold Schwarzenegger in 1986. Their marriage has gracefully endured two decades of seismic shifts: dramatic career changes, superstardom, the birth of four children and political activism. Shriver supported her husband in his successful run for California governor in late 2003.

In early 2004, Shriver announced she would step down from her full-time job with NBC News to focus on her role as first lady of California, though she continues working on occasional TV projects.

Shriver is the author of the self-help book *Ten Things I Wish I'd Known—Before I Went Into the Real World* (2000).

In 2001, she authored a children's book about disabilities *What's Wrong With Timmy?* Her most recent book, *What's Wrong With Grandpa?*, was sparked from her desire to help her children understand her father's battle with Alzheimer's.

A truly elegant combination of style and substance, Maria Shriver calls herself a "work in progress" and even chafes at the old-fashioned title—first lady—a title her famous aunt Jacqueline Kennedy Onassis once compared to being called a "saddle horse."

www.msnbc.com/onair/bios/m_shriver.asp

www.who2.com/mariashriver.html

Ten Things I Wish I'd Known - Before I Went Into the Real World

What's Wrong with Timmy

93. Michael Crichton

Born in 1942 in Chicago, Illinois, USA

Occupation: author, director

Claim to Fame: blockbuster books and movies

Achievements: Michael is the only person to have had the number-one book, number-one movie and number-one television show in the U.S., all at the same time; won an Emmy, a Peabody and a Writer's Guild of America award for *ER;* named one of the "Fifty Most Beautiful People" by *People* magazine in 1992

Story: Michael Crichton became a best-selling novelist after graduating from Harvard Medical School. The story goes that every year of medical school he tried to quit, and each time he was persuaded to give it another try. He paid his way through Harvard by writing thrillers that had to be published under pen names so as not to disturb the upstanding medical community.

Many of his books and films have achieved blockbuster status, and he's known as "the father of the techno-thriller." His long list of credits includes *The Andromeda Strain, Congo, Jurassic Park* and *Timeline.*

His books have been translated into thirty languages. Twelve have been made into films. He's also the creator of the award-winning television series *ER.*

Crichton has directed six films, among them *Westworld*, which is distinguished as the first feature film to use computer-generated special effects. Obviously, he pioneered a trend that has become ubiquitous in today's movie production. He won an Academy of Motion Pictures Arts and Sciences Technical Achievement Award in 1995 for his work in this area.

www.randomhouse.com/features/crichton/bio.html

www.globalnets.com/crichton/left/bio.html

Travels

Michael Crichton: A New Collection of Three Complete Novels

94. Dr. Sally Ride

Born in 1951 in Los Angeles, California, USA

Occupation: astronaut, physicist

Claim to Fame: first American woman in space

Obstacles Faced: being a female pioneer in a traditionally male occupation

Achievements: inducted into the Astronaut Hall of Fame at Kennedy Space Center in June 2003, awarded the Jefferson Award for Public Service, twice been awarded the National Spaceflight Medal

Story: After earning her Master of Science and doctorate degrees in physics from Stanford in 1975 and 1978, Dr. Sally Ride was selected for astronaut training in and reported for duty to NASA. She was a member of the support crew for both the second and third space shuttle flights and worked in mission control. Ride was not destined to remain earthbound, however, and became one of the handful of human beings to experience outer space.

Dr. Ride has been in space twice, aboard the Challenger space shuttle, first in 1983 and again in 1984. The plan for her third space flight was grounded by the tragic Challenger accident in 1986, an event that many of us witnessed on television. Instead of heading back out into space, Ride spent the next six months investigating the accident as a member of the Presidential Commission.

In 1987, Ride retired from NASA in order to join the team at the Center for International Security and Arms Control at Stanford University as a Science Fellow. She was also the Director of the California Space Science Institute, a research institute of the University of California.

Today Dr. Ride is a member of the faculty at the University of California as a physics professor. She also serves on the President's Committee of Advisors on Science and Technology.

An advocate for young women entering the sciences, she regularly lectures and writes on the necessity of girls to study math and science. For her efforts, she earned the Women's Research and Education Institute's American Woman Award.

www.jsc.nasa.gov/Bios/htmlbios/ride-sk.html
www.imaginarylinesinc.com
To Space and Back

95. Senator Elizabeth Dole

Born in 1936 in Salisbury, North Carolina, USA

Occupation: U.S. senator from North Carolina

Claim to Fame: the only woman who has served as a cabinet secretary for two federal departments and under two presidents; formed an exploratory committee to run for the presidency in 2000, but withdrew from the race on October 29, 1999—the election was won by George W. Bush

Obstacles Faced: being a woman in the boy's club of Washington from 1960 to today, husband's bout with cancer

Achievements: few men or women have matched Elizabeth Dole's success in Washington; named "North Carolinian of the Year" by the North Carolina Press Association in 1993; Women Executives in State Government honored Dole with its Lifetime Achievement Award in 1993; received the Humanitarian Award from the National Commission Against Drunk Driving in 1998

Family: married Bob Dole in December 1975, creating one of Washington's most famous power couples; they have one daughter, Robin

Story: Senator Dole was formerly employed in President Lyndon Johnson's White House and as deputy assistant to President Richard M. Nixon and to President Ronald Reagan. Dole served as president of the American Red Cross from 1991 through 1999. She currently serves as the national director of Education and Information for Hospice.

Voted Most Likely to Succeed when she graduated from high school, Dole graduated with distinction from Duke University in 1958, earned a degree from Harvard Law School in 1965 and also holds a master's degree in education and government from Harvard. In 1967, she worked for a public interest law firm and then stepped into the political arena, where she blazed a prominent trail.

Originally a Democrat, then an Independent, Elizabeth switched her party registration upon marrying Bob Dole and became a Republican.

www.senate.gov/pagelayout/senators/one_item_and_teasers/dole.htm

Hearts Touched by Fire: My 500 Most Inspirational Quotations

Elizabeth Dole (Women of Achievement)

96. General Norman Schwarzkopf

Born in 1934 in Trenton, New Jersey, USA

Occupation: former American Army general

Claim to Fame: best known for his services as Commander, United States Central Command and Commander of Operations of Desert Shield and Desert Storm

Obstacles Faced: in 1971, returned home from his second tour of duty in Vietnam in a hip-to-shoulder body cast due to his injuries

Achievements: decorations include five Distinguished Service Medals, three Silver Stars, the Bronze Star, the Purple Heart, the Presidential Medal of Freedom, the National Order of the Legion of Honor and decorations from France, Belgium, the United Kingdom, Bahrain, Qatar, the United Arab Emirates, Saudi Arabia and Kuwait

Family: married, with three children

Story: Son of a Brigadier General, Norman Schwarzkopf graduated from West Point in 1956 with a Bachelor's of Science in mechanical engineering, as a 2nd Lieutenant. He then earned a Master's degree in Mechanical Engineering at the University of Southern California.

During his years of service, he commanded Army units from platoon through corps level. He served two combat tours in the Republic of Vietnam, where he was wounded twice and repeatedly decorated for bravery. Later, he was designated the Deputy Commander of the Joint Task Force in charge of U.S. forces participating in the Grenada student rescue operation. He's fondly called "Storm'n Norman."

Most famous for his position as Commander of America's Operation Desert Storm, he helped the U.S. prevail in the Gulf War. Schwarzkopf retired from the Army in 1992 and wrote his autobiography *It Doesn't Take a Hero.*

General Schwarzkopf is in great demand as a public speaker and in recent years has used his fame to raise public awareness of prostate cancer.

www.usdreams.com/Schwarzkopf.html

www.achievement.org/autodoc/page/sch0pro-1

It Doesn't Take a Hero: The Autobiography of General H. Norman Schwarzkopf

In the Eye of the Storm: the Life of General H. Norman Schwarzkopf

97. Senator Bob Dole

Born in 1936 in Russell, Kansas, USA

Occupation: former attorney, congressman, senator (Kansas) and Republican presidential candidate

Claim to Fame: one of the most powerful senators of our time, as well as a decorated war hero; in 1996, won GOP nomination for president

Obstacles Faced: disabled by injuries received during World War II, while rescuing fallen comrades; overcame prostate cancer

Achievements: elected to the House of Representatives in 1960, 1962, 1964, 1966; became senator for Kansas in November 1968; re-elected in 1974, 1980, 1988, 1992; from 1983-1999, president of the Dole Foundation, a non-profit, grant-giving organization he founded which dealt with disability issues; holds the Chairmanship of the International Commission on Missing Persons and of the National World War II Memorial; in January 2003, appointed Honorary Co-Chair of the President's Council on Service and Civic Participation, part of President Bush's USA Freedom Corps; twice decorated for heroic achievement in WWII, receiving two Purple Hearts and the Bronze Star; in 1997, awarded the Presidential Medal of Freedom as a tribute to his character and contributions to the nation

Family: married to The Honorable Elizabeth Hanford Dole, current senator from North Carolina; they have one daughter, Robin

Story: Bob Dole is an icon in the American political arena, respected by all parties for his hard work, legislative brilliance, exemplary career, philanthropy and dedication to charitable causes. He was decorated during WWII for acts of bravery above and beyond the call of duty while suffering from injuries. He continues to struggle with pain and disability due to those injuries.

After building an impressive record as an attorney, Dole successfully ran for congress and later elected to the senate. In 1996, he said an emotional farewell and resigned from the U.S. Senate to devote all of his time and energy to his campaign for president.

www.bobdole.org

Great Political Wit: Laughing (Almost) All the Way to the White House

Great Presidential Wit (...I Wish I Was in the Book): A Collection of Humorous Anecdotes and Quotations

98. Bill O'Reilly

Born in 1949 in New York City, USA

Occupation: journalist, anchor, producer, reporter

Claim to Fame: highest-ranked cable news show in America

Achievements: awarded two Emmy Awards for Excellence in Reporting; won two National Headliner Awards for news reporting for the ABC network; honored by The National Academy of Arts and Sciences for his reporting and analysis on and after September 11, 2001

Family: married, with two children

Story: Bill O'Reilly navigated his road to the top of his profession by starting with an extensive education. He earned a history degree, a Master's degree in broadcast journalism from Boston University and a Master's degree in Public Administration from Harvard's Kennedy School of Government. From there, he steered a sure course through local news stations into the big leagues of broadcast news.

In 1980, O'Reilly hosted a nightly TV magazine show at CBS. In 1986, he joined ABC and won awards for his reporting. In 1989, he was the host of *Inside Edition*, which enjoyed considerable success with O'Reilly at the helm. He was hired in 1996 by the new Fox News Channel for his signature segment, *The O'Reilly Report*.

Now called *The O'Reilly Factor*, his show dominates television news ratings in America and has been ranked the highest cable news show for two years. Expanding his mediums, O'Reilly took on radio in 2002, with one of the most successful syndicated radio shows ever—The Radio Factor.

In the publishing world, he dominates as well. O'Reilly is one of only two authors in the past ten years to have three consecutive number-one, non-fiction books on the *New York Times* best-seller list. *The O'Reilly Factor*, *The No Spin Zone* and *Who's Looking Out for You* have sold millions of copies worldwide.

www.billoreilly.com

www.foxnews.com/story/0,2933,155,00.html

Who's Looking Out for You?

The O'Reilly Factor: The Good, the Bad, and the Completely Ridiculous in American Life

The No-Spin Zone: Confrontations with the Powerful and Famous in America

99. Meg Whitman

Born 1957 in New York City, USA

Occupation: president of eBay

Claim to Fame: the force behind the consumer phenomenon eBay.com

Obstacles Faced: internet auction buying and selling was nonexistent when she began

Achievements: one of only two female CEOs of Fortune 500 companies; among Whitman's many accolades, *Fortune* magazine ranked her the third most powerful woman in business in 2002; *Worth* magazine ranked her number one on its 2002 list of best CEOs; and *Business Week* named her among the 25 most powerful business managers annually since 2000

Family: married, with two sons

Story: Nothing succeeds like success. And nothing succeeds like helping others succeed. That's the secret behind eBay and the motto of its president Meg Whitman.

eBay is the world's online marketplace and the number-one consumer e-commerce site. The meteoric success of eBay, a brilliant idea turned respected business, is due to two things. First is the willingness and passion of millions of ordinary people to buy and sell virtually *anything* at the user-friendly site. The second is the new queen of dot com, Meg Whitman.

Whitman joined eBay as president and CEO in March 1998. Her expertise in brand building, combined with her passion for creating exceptional consumer experiences, helped eBay evolve into a leading company, altering how commerce takes place around the world.

Meg sits on the Board of Directors of Procter & Gamble and Princeton University Board of Trustees. She received a Bachelor of Economics from Princeton University and an M.B.A. from Harvard Business School.

Although women make up almost half of America's labor force, only two Fortune 500 companies have women CEOs or presidents. Whitman's achievements are an inspiration to a new generation of women.

 www.pages.ebay.com/community/aboutebay/overview/management.html

100. Rupert Murdoch

Born in 1931 in Melbourne, Australia; became an American citizen in 1985

Occupation: media tycoon

Claim to Fame: owner of some of the world's most notable newspapers and media outlets through his News Corporation company

Achievements: his media conglomerate has ventures in all forms of media: television, film, print and the Internet; owns 20th Century Fox, The Fox Network, HarperCollins and *The New York Post,* among dozens of others

Family: married to second wife, 40 years his junior; resides in Manhattan; four children from a previous marriage

Story: Rupert Murdoch, the world's biggest media mogul, owns the majority of the newspaper industry in Australia, Britain and North America, Europe and Asia. CEO of a company with a net worth of over $5 billion, Murdoch's true power is in his influence.

With a major interest in the message, along with control over the medium, it's fair to say that mainstream interpretation of world events and issues is filtered through Murdoch's lens.

Satellite television, movies, news outlets, newspapers, magazines, websites and book publishing are all part of Murdoch's domain, which he leads with a famously firm hand and right-wing perspective. Murdoch is often courted by politicians to convince him to favorably cover their campaigns.

www.askmen.com/men/business_politics/27c_rupert_murdoch.html
www.woopidoo.com/biography/rupert-murdoch.htm
The Murdoch Mission: The Digital Transformation of a Media Empire
Big Shots: Business the Rupert Murdoch Way

101. Tom Hanks

Born in 1956 in California, USA

Occupation: actor, director, producer

Claim to Fame: named Favorite All-Time Entertainer by the People's Choice Awards in 2004

Obstacles Faced: unstable childhood

Achievements: a record-breaking series of blockbuster movies, named #9 on *Forbes* Top 100 Celebrity list in 2003, earned 45 awards since 1988

Family: divorced, with two children from previous marriage; married to Rita Wilson, with two children; is a direct descendant of Nancy Hanks, Abraham Lincoln's mother

Story: Remember *Big, The Green Mile, Saving Private Ryan, You've Got Mail, Apollo 13, Toy Story, Forrest Gump, Philadelphia, Sleepless in Seattle,* and *Castaway*? Tom Hanks is likely why you remember. He's one of the most respected, likable and bankable men in Hollywood. According to *Entertainment Weekly,* he has a winning streak of 10 consecutive movies in which he has starred that grossed over $100 million domestically in the U.S. That's a record.

While majoring in theater at California State University, Hanks was recruited by the Great Lakes Shakespeare Festival in Ohio after an outstanding school performance. After three years with the Shakespeare festival, he headed to the Big Apple with big dreams. After a couple of mediocre film and television roles, he landed the lead in Ron Howard's *Splash.*

He really hit it big with *Big,* the 1988 comedy that helped him step up out of the B-list of actors. Finally, in 1993, Hanks became an A-list actor and an Oscar favorite, while winning the hearts of women everywhere in *Sleepless in Seattle* and the hearts of everyone as an AIDS victim in *Philadelphia.* He won the Academy Award for Best Actor that year and picked up the gold statue once again for his title role in *Forrest Gump* the following year.

Truly a multi-faceted talent, Hanks has put his hand to scriptwriting, directing and producing.

www.askmen.com

Tom Hanks: The Unauthorized Biography

What's *Your* Best Advice?

We asked our 101 Most Successful People Living Today what they would offer for advice in getting ahead in the world. This is the question we asked them:

> *"What advice would you give a son, daughter or grandchild? Based upon your knowledge and experience, what would you share with them that would be most helpful to them getting along and getting ahead in the world?"*

The answers have been fascinating and comprise the heart of this book.

But what would *you* say if you had the chance? What do you consider to be the most profound advice you could share with someone you love? How would you impress upon this young person the importance of your wisdom?

Please tell us. It might even make it into the *next* book. Perhaps we'll have to create another 101 Best book: "Sage SuccessNet Subscribers Share their Success Strategies"!

Send your responses to 101BestAdvice@SuccessNet.org

Appendix

Recommended Resources

☐ *101 Best Experts—Who Help Us Improve Our Lives*
www.SuccessNet.org/go/101experts.htm

☐ AwakenTheAuthorWithin.com
Author an eBook in Record Time
www.SuccessNet.org/go/awakenauthor.htm

☐ *One Minute Millionaire* (free with CD)
www.SuccessNet.org/go/1mm.htm

☐ Philip Humbert - Resources for Success
www.SuccessNet.org/humbert.htm

☐ Self Help Salon
www.SuccessNet.org/go/selfhelpsalon.htm

☐ Sterling Valentine – Winning the Client Game
www.SterlingValentine.com

☐ SuccessNet Membership
www.SuccessNet.org/join.htm

☐ What in the Heck is Success Anyway?
www.SuccessNet.org/articles/wsuccess.htm

Other Products and Services Available from SuccessNet

☐ *101 Things I've Learned in My 50 Trips Around the Sun* (free)
www.SuccessNet.org/reports.htm

☐ *101 Ways to Save Time and Be More Effective*
www.SuccessNet.org/101savetime.htm

☐ *Success Teams* (free)
www.SuccessNet.org/files/teams.pdf

☐ Freedom to Achieve™ System
www.SuccessNet.org/fta/

☐ Laser Questions™
www.SuccessNet.org/laserq.htm

☐ Priorities™
www.SuccessNet.org/priorities.htm

☐ Quotation Library
www.SuccessNet.org/library.htm

☐ *Strategies for Success* eBook
www.SuccessNet.org/book.htm

☐ *Success: A Spiritual Matter*
www.SuccessNet.org/spirit/

☐ World Class Business™ Conference
Take your business to the next level
www.WorldClassBusiness.com

☐ Your Core Values™ eCourse
www.YourCoreValues.com

☐ www.CreatingExcellence.com
Daily motivation and inspiration to help you excel.
For employers and employees who want to make every day
more productive and fulfilling.

The Invitation Letter to the 101 Most Successful

This is the letter we sent to the people who our readers selected as the most successful:

Congratulations. According to our subscribers and members from around the globe (nearly 100,000 strong), **you're seen as one of the most successful people in the world.**

As founder and president of SuccessNet, I've dedicated myself to helping people operate at their personal and professional best by providing publications, resources, conferences and an online community since 1995. Like you, I strive every day to make a positive difference in the lives of as many people as possible.

We recently surveyed our readers and asked them to submit the names of five people they consider the most successful and respected living today. You were ranked in the top 101.

Certainly, your contribution to the world is significant. You're someone people look to as a source of inspiration and advice. Thousands of our readers thought so.

The list of 101 most successful and respected individuals has the potential for helping tens of thousands of people in a unique way. That's why I plan to compile advice from you and the other 100.

In the next few weeks, we're publishing a book called "101 Ways to Get Ahead—solid gold advice from 101 of the most successful people in the world". It will include words of wisdom, encouragement and advice for anyone with a desire to build a better life and more fully realize their potential. Your advice will be a significant addition to the book.

My request is that you become an integral part of this project by contributing up to three pieces of advice that you'd most want to impart to others. In addition, we'd appreciate a brief bio of your life and accomplishments.

Imagine if you had a moment with someone near and dear to you— a niece or nephew, a grandchild, a friend—what advice would you most want to offer them? In your experience, what advice would most support an individual in pursuing their dreams, overcoming obstacles and living up to their potential?

Your advice will be included in the book, along with a bio of your life and accomplishments. And, of course, we'll send you a copy of the finished book.

I hope you'll look at this request for your valuable time and advice as an opportunity to impart some of your knowledge and experience to others. By sharing your best advice on achieving success, you'll be reaching out to tens of thousands who endeavor to make a lasting difference in the world.

We've been in business for over eight years and have developed an excellent reputation for producing valuable and trustworthy information. We promise to do our best in creating a book that represents you and your knowledge in the very best light.

Thank you. And make it a great day.

Michael E. Angier, CIO (Chief Inspirational Officer)

About SuccessNet

SuccessNet is an international association of people committed to operating at their best—to creating excellence in every aspect of their lives and throughout their respective organizations. We support people in developing the skills, knowledge, belief and passion to achieve their dreams.

> OUR MISSION:
> to inform, inspire and empower people to be their best—personally and professionally.

SuccessNet is dedicated to helping you become more knowledgeable, prosperous and effective. In addition to our publications, we provide a complete membership package dedicated to making your road to success easier and more fun.

Since 1995, over 150,000 people from all around the globe have benefited from the SuccessNet experience.

People from all walks of life become members: small-business owners, managers and people who want to get ahead in their careers. Anyone who wants to maximize their potential, improve the quality of their lives and make a lasting difference in the world.

SuccessNet is for great people who want to become even better.

Free Subscription
Subscribe at www.SuccessNet.org/mem_app.htm or by sending an email to subscribe@SuccessNet.org

You'll also be enrolled in the free seven-lesson *Step up to Success Course*™.

Visit our web site at www.successnet.org

Success Networks International
Win-Win Way, PO Box 2048
So Burlington, Vermont 05407-2048 USA
802.862.0812

The SuccessNet Creed

The principles and beliefs upon which SuccessNet was founded and the guidelines by which it operates.

WE BELIEVE we have a responsibility—a sacred trust—to conduct business with the utmost integrity and with impeccable ethics. We further believe that this responsibility goes beyond mere legality and encompasses a sense of fair play for all involved. We play win-win and we play it well.

WE BELIEVE that a balanced life is the only life worth living. Without it, no real fulfillment can be experienced. Having financial success at the expense of one's health or one's family is not true success. We recognize that striking this balance is not easy.

WE BELIEVE success is indeed a journey and not a destination—that it's not what we achieve, but rather what we *become* in the process of our achievements. It's not what happens *to* us but what we do about what happens to us that makes the difference.

WE BELIEVE we must give in order to receive—that if we help enough other people get what they want, we can get what we want. We commit to serving and supporting others—to helping them realize their potential and, in the process, realize our own.

WE BELIEVE in dreams—that all great achievements in history came from the pursuit of a dream, and that it's incumbent upon us to discover, honor and fulfill the dreams we have within us.

WE BELIEVE that clarity leads to power. When we're clear on our objectives, know what our core values are and consistently focus on the things that matter, we really can accomplish anything we choose.

WE BELIEVE in the resilience and potential of the human spirit, that men and women are created in the image of God and that we're capable of accomplishing anything—although not necessarily *everything*— we set out to do.

WE BELIEVE business is all about relationships with people—that good business is built by creating relationships of trust, by keeping agreements and maintaining integrity.

WE BELIEVE that commerce has been and will continue to be a primary influence in world issues and that world peace is furthered by strong and interrelated business alliances. As business and people become more interdependent upon one another, we become freer and decrease the likelihood of armed conflict because we recognize it's impossible to sink half the ship.

WE BELIEVE that by providing excellent products and services, people will reward us with their business. When we promise a lot and deliver even more, we secure the loyalty and patronage of the consumer. We commit to constant and never-ending improvement of what we offer our customers.

WE BELIEVE the path of mastery is through the joy of creating excellence in all that we do and the way in which we do it. When we do what we love, we're not only happier, we produce better products and services.

WE BELIEVE every customer, employee, stockholder, servant, competitor and partner is first and foremost a person—a unique expression of Universal Spirit—someone who deserves our respect and consideration.

WE BELIEVE that change is not only inevitable but good; not only unpredictable, but also stimulating and educational. It's rarely comfortable, but it's essential to our growth and development. Accepting change and adapting to it will always win out over resistance.

WE BELIEVE mistakes and failures are an integral and necessary part of success and embrace them as learning experiences.

WE BELIEVE the use of knowledge is power and we are committed to our own ongoing educational process. We further believe that our knowledge is to always be used for good—never to cause harm.

WE BELIEVE that information, information technologies and the sharing of same creates more freedom. It levels the playing field, thereby reducing injustice and making it more difficult for tyranny, prejudice, misunderstanding and inequality to reign.

Index of The 101 Most Successful (listed by last name)

Printed in the United States
29216LVS00001B/235-267